D1226514

INVITATION TO A DIALOGUE

INVITATION TO A DIALOGUE

Union and Separation in Family Life

By
OTTO POLLAK
University of Pennsylvania
and
ELLEN S. WISE
Children's Hospital of Pennsylvania

SP MEDICAL & SCIENTIFIC BOOKS
New York • London

SPECTRUM PUBLICATIONS, INC.
175-20 Wexford Terrace, Jamaica, N.Y. 11432

Library of Congress Cataloging in Publication Data

Pollack, Otto, 1908–
    Invitation to a dialogue.

    Includes index.
    1. Family. 2. Life cycle, Human. 3. Pain.
4. Pleasure. I. Wise, Ellen S., joint author.
II. Title.
HQ734.P744   301.42   79-19154
ISBN 0-89335-081-8

*To those whom we love
and from whom we have learned*

Contents

Preface

The book presented tries to trace the experience of family life by
an individual from birth to death. It is written in the developmental
framework and differs from many texts by avoiding statistics and
trans-cultural comparisons. The underlying philosophy is existentialism. The psychological key concepts are taken from *Two Essays
on Analytical Psychology* by C. G. Jung. The sociological orientation is geared to social change as we experience it in the second half
of the Twentieth Century with emphasis on the Women's Movement.

Introduction

In this book we present a philosophy of family life in the belief that a life without any philosophical orientation is unbecoming to human dignity and prevents people from coping with adversity through their own strength. Although many of the phenomena we will discuss are familiar, the interconnections between apparently independent experiences are often overlooked or taken for granted. The interconnections which we invite our readers to study and understand are essentially the bipolar qualities of family life, such as comfort and discomfort, loss and gain, constraint and liberation, security and challenge, and, most important, union and separation. We believe that these apparently contradictory experiences are actually meaningful and ultimately connected in a rewarding way. We would not know comfort if we had not experienced discomfort, or be aware of gain if we had not experienced loss. We would not know the relief of liberation if we had not been confined within limiting care by our parents and, in adulthood, by the prison of an unhappy marriage. On the other hand, we would not recognize the support of limiting care or the joy and security of a good marriage if we had not encountered the dread of being unattended in the limitless desert of an unstructured world.

We mean to show further that these connections between bipolar phenomena repeat themselves throughout the life cycle so that for most of its span we meet not the unknown but rather, old experiences in new shapes and new sizes. We believe this recognition provides strengthening and a basis of hope and courage. Our experiences teach us to live from stage to stage of our life cycle if we are able to comprehend the lessons. They will do so, however, only if we learn to discard our fantasies of permanent solutions and to accept the relentless demand for ever-new adaptations. The basic experiences repeat themselves, but the methods of coping with them in family life present ever-new challenges. The adaptive response to these challenges is the recognition that what seems to be new has existed before (*plus ça change, plus c'est la même chose*) and to learn from this experience.

Our philosophical approach to the phenomenon of family life is reflected in the joint undertaking of the writing of this book by an old man and a young woman. Our co-authorship enabled us to combine in our search for meaningful connections the bipolar experiences of different sexes and generations. In this way we tried to take a first step toward a challenge of the disbelief of so many authors that any one person alone can understand, on the basis of his or her experiences, the totality of the human condition. Rather than assuming the counterposition that only a multitude of authors contributing to an anthology can effectively communicate such a totality, every chapter in this book is the result of a dialogue between the authors.

In our dialogues we have identified the central themes of family life with particular emphasis on the ever recurring problems of union and separation. There is, however, another dialogue which should be conducted: the dialogue between the authors of the book and the readers. It will be up to the reader in his silent responses to the text of our book to validate the philosophy that we present. The book requires, therefore, an active readership. We challenge the reader to confirm or refute our statements. These statements are not tentative in our conviction, but, of course, they are not validated by our conviction. This can be done only by the echo of experience which they produce in the reader.

The phenomena we have identified and their interconnections are presented with a claim to universality at least within the bounds of our culture. Our intention has been to write for different ages and sexes within the range of this culture. We believe that many statements in our book will ring true to our readers. Our propositions would probably strike a responding chord in many people who will never read the book but that, of course, is in the realm of the unprovable. If our readers can experientially validate just one statement in the book or whatever their experiential range covers, we think we may reasonably expect that they will give us credibility for that range of experiences unfamiliar to them. We span the experiences of both sexes as well as the period of maturation and development from childhood to old age. We expect readers to fall somewhere within these dimensions. They cannot help, therefore, to have at least partial competence for validation or refutation of statements.

It is our hope that young people especially will read our book and will consider not only their present condition but also what lies ahead of them. Their future experiences are currently the present of their elders. On this basis we hope not only to evoke a dialogue with our readers but also a continuous dialogue between them and their families about the never ending and always interesting issues of their life together.

We live in times when we fight the realities of the human condition—such as aging, boundaries of the human potential, and the repetitive experience of union and separation—and we find ourselves in a constant state of disappointment. We shall try to present a philosophy which might correct this currently prevalent experience of discomfort and dissatisfaction with universal realities by stressing their bipolarity. Resistance to the acceptance of the human condition obscures certain important aspects of life and, by so doing, makes life an unhappy experience rather than a source of gratification.

We believe that one need not be ideally situated in family life to get a great deal of meaning and satisfaction out of it. The same is true for physical and mental health. People with physical impairments or chronic diseases may lead otherwise satisfactory lives. Neurotic people may find important areas of living unaffected by their disabilities and gain in these areas support for self esteem and a feeling of worthwhileness. But the misery of the depressed is global and pessimistic and we hope that our book may be of particular help to them.

We raise the issue of pain and release from pain as a necessary interconnection. A permanently well individual would not even be aware of this condition because he would have no basis of comparison for formulating a judgment. A person continually in pain would be aware of his condition but such awareness would have no positive effects because pain without hope for relief is exhausting and can ultimately lead to suicide. We can only have awareness and experience of happiness in the middle area between pain and release from pain and in anticipatory experiences. In pain we are sustained by hope of relief; in relief we are sustained by the hope that if we should lose it we will be able to cope with new pain in the expectation of new relief. Our awareness of happiness depends upon its intermittent nature. In this respect our book is an affirmative one because its essential message is that the pain described by so many other authors is a phenomenon that is not only intermittent but necessary if we are to experience happiness in the family when we start one and when we continue to stay in it.

A philosopher might raise the question, "Why, if this intermittent experience of pain and relief from pain is the human condition, haven't people been more effective in coping with it and benefiting from it?" The answer lies in the feeling of injury and injustice which people connect with pain. They dwell on it and become preoccupied with it. Well-being, on the other hand, the state of life "as it is supposed to be" is frequently taken for granted and represents no object of reflection. To counteract this tendency to become oblivious of well-being, we shall try to show why family life is necessarily a succession of painful experiences and relief, not how to avoid this essential nature of it. The reader who would believe that the book is redundant would be mistaken. Life is redundant.

Our procedure will be not only to describe the ideal situation during each stage of the life cycle, but also the inevitable reality of each stage. We will describe how things can go wrong at every stage of development and will try to explain why. Perhaps we can suggest ways to cope through an understanding of the dynamics of human development, but we do not promise any utopian solution because any such promise would contradict our thesis of the interconnection between pain and release. The invitation to join us in our dialogue is based on the belief that its acceptance can have an influence on the reader's life. If we felt it could have no such influence, we would be hard pressed to find a justification for extending the invitation. It is our hope that when people read this book a mythology that life can and should be permanently satisfactory will be destroyed or at least attacked—because this mythology dooms people to disappointment. The evaluation of any experience is bound to have a negative outcome if the expectations of positive outcome are exaggerated.

As mentioned before, it is an unfortunate tendency of our time to focus on pain rather than on satisfaction. Simultaneously we search for utopias and encounter of necessity failure after failure. These two tendencies distort our outlook on family life as well as on other areas of the human experience. We are pessimists in perception and optimists in expectations. In this book we try to fight this unfortunate combination.

The Authors

SUGGESTED READINGS

John Bowlby, *Attachment and Loss*. New York, Basic Books, 1969.

David Cooper, *The Death of the Family*. New York, Pantheon Books, Random House, 1970.

H.V. Dichs, *Marital Tension*. New York, Basic Books, 1967.

Sigmund Freud, *The Complete Introductory Lectures on Psychoanalysis*. New York, W. W. Norton, 1966.

Heinz Hartmann, *Ego Psychology and the Problem of Adaptation*. New York, International Universities Press, 1958.

C. G. Jung, *Two Essays on Analytical Psychology*. Bollinger Series XX Princeton University Press, Second Ed., 1972

Theodore Lidz, *Person: His Development Throughout the Life Cycle*. New York, Basic Books, 1968.

James Leslie McCary, *Freedom and Growth in Marriage*. Santa Barbara, Hamilton Publishing Company, 1975.

Margaret S. Mahler, *On Human Symbiosis and the Vicissitudes of the Individual*. New York, International Universities Press, 1966.

H. Sterling, *Conflict and Reconciliation*. Garden City, N.Y., Doubleday Anchor Books, 1969.

Part I

Anatomy, Experience
and Coping

CHAPTER 1

Biological Destiny, Psychological Evaluation, and Social Implications

The advances of modern technology and the public debate over women's claim to equal representation in the labor force and to equal rewards have obscured the fact that *anatomy is still destiny.* Being male or female means still and probably always will mean that one has a body which is differently built than the body of the other gender and that in the area of sexual experiences, maturation and aging one has different experiences. This phenomenon of difference is not subject to change by social action. Every human being must cope with it in encounters with a person of the other gender and frequently in self evaluation. It is anatomical destiny that people experience their organism as incomplete when compared with the organism of the other sex.

The process of birth represents a violent and painful ejection of the fetus by the body of the mother. The umbilical cord still connecting mother and child must be cut. Two lives that were one are separated and, if the child is male, are separated from one another not only as bodies but also by anatomical, physiological, psychological and developmental differences. Even if it is a girl, the developmental differences between her and her mother will persist and change in both individuals will put them over and over again into different stages of maturation and aging. Thus, separation and difference are permanent parts of the human experience and throughout the life cycle people try to undo their differences and

3

separation by a striving for wholeness and union. They do it in the symbiotic relationship of mother and child in the first year of the child's life; they do it throughout childhood in trying to establish a closeness with the father, with siblings, with teachers and schoolmates; they continue to do it in love relationship, in marriage; in illness they search for it in their relationship with physicians and nurses until death puts an end to the search for union and the experience of separation. From this point of view, the total experience of a human being in family life can be seen as a sequence of fluctuations between the two stages of separation and union. People are over and over again coping with physical, psychological, and even geographical separation. Their ability to form unions, resolve unions, and form new unions prevents separation from driving people to despair.

Still, going through the life cycle requires more. Human beings need also optimism, fortitude, and generosity. One must offer closeness, one must let people go, one must find new closeness in various degrees of intensity, and one must ultimately face the fact that there is no lasting reward for all this striving because in death there is "nothingness."

Perhaps the strongest expression of the fact that anatomy is destiny is the phenomenon of maturation and decline. People are born unfinished and helpless. Given a measure of care and service, they will mature and complete the development of their sexual identity through the appearance of secondary sex characteristics; the relative lack of differentiation in the bodies of the young—absence of breasts in the girl, absence of hair on the face of the boy, absence of pubic hair in children of both sexes—will disappear. The human being will attain maturity—and begin to lose it. As the body declines, reminders of bisexuality will occur; women will discover hair growth on their faces; men will discover a sagging in their chest tissues which will approach breast development; pubic hair will become less luxuriant in both sexes. Men and women decline into similarity and into eventual death.

Perhaps the most overwhelming experience, short of the awareness that life runs toward its own ultimate destruction, is the experience of being born female or male. The female body is an enigma to the woman herself as well as to men. The female sex organs are not outwardly visible and the response in a sexual encounter can be pretended without being experienced. The experience of the menstrual cycle represents a specific burden for which a young girl is not prepared by a slow process of maturation. Its onset is dramatic and its ending similarly so. The experience of pregnancy and childbirth with their discomforts and pain, the experience of the menopause with its hot flashes and the loss of the experience of the cycle, make femaleness a specific experience of half of humankind to which men have only partial observational access. The genital equipment of women is essentially receptive, an equipment which may not always be experienced as appropriate in terms of one's feelings and dispositions.

The male body, however, is equipped for an invasive sex act which may not be in harmony with the feelings and predispositions of all human beings so equipped. The male sex organs are clearly visible. There is no mystery about them: they are accessible to visual perception by self and others. Men are unable to conceal physical arousal as well as lack of it and it is difficult for veracity to be exposed to an enigma: the male can never really know how a woman reacts to him in the sex act, whereas a female can never be uncertain as to her partner's arousal. There are probably many males who enter the sex act with the anxiety of exposure of sexual inadequacy and many females who are free of such anxiety because their anatomy protects any non-responsiveness that may occur. In one respect, however, anatomy is kinder to man than to woman. Sexual decline is slower, less dramatic, and not conspicuously tied to a specific decade in the life cycle.

The pessimist could say that the essence of all development is a replacement of old discomforts by new ones. This replacement has two dimensions; what one has learned to cope with is replaced by experiences which one has not yet learned to manage. These new experiences require the development of new coping patterns which, in turn, will become obsolete with further development. There is, therefore, in all maturation an element of restlessness which is accompanied by feelings of uncertainty and fatigue.

The second dimension of development is the polarity between success and failure in coping. One becomes aware of one's own sexual identity in encounters with the opposite sex in which one

can use one's sex according to one's biological potential, or fail to
use it. It may require time and experimentation to learn such uses
or to overcome such failures.

In the encounter one may discover dissatisfaction with one's own
sex because it imposes upon one the burden of learning to live with
difference. It deprives one of the feeling of security that comes from
encounters with similarity. Another source of dissatisfaction with
one's own sex is not only the predicament of having to learn to live
with difference but the evaluation of how well one learns to do it.
Women may not find themselves beautiful enough; men may not
find themselves strong enough. Many people are embarrassed by
being too tall, and others by being too short.

Therefore, having to live with people who are essentially different produces by definition an element of antagonism between the
sexes. It makes life more difficult to have to live with somebody
whom one cannot fully understand. It may be difficult to live with
somebody who understands you better than you understand him
or her. Difference is annoying because it challenges you and you do
not know whether you can ever meet the challenge. This uncertainty makes one angry with oneself, with one's limitations and
with having to continue to respond to the challenges of life with
inadequate equipment. Frequently, the anger with self may be
displaced and directed against other persons, against social conditions, or even against human destiny as such. It is easier to bear
anger with others than anger with self. Anger with others has an
element of righteousness. Given social inequalities, it finds rationalization in social conditions. Although it may seem that the anger
of males and females is directed at one another, in the last analysis
it is anger with oneself, anger based on the nonacceptance of the
limitations and problems forced upon oneself by one's anatomical
destiny.

Fortunately anger is not the only response to difference. Positively speaking, difference is a challenge to the overcoming of one's
own disabilities, to the relief of separation by the attainment of at
least temporary union with a lover, a spouse, or generally with
other human beings in meaningful relationships. Although no
union can be maintained forever, neither need separation be
endured without attempts to form new unions, be this with the

same person or another. The life span is full of periods of unions and separations, and one never needs to feel that one is imprisoned by the former or doomed to suffer the latter. Only in cases of pathology will people resist the shifts from one to the other. Children need the experience of both the security of union and the liberation of separation; so do adults and so do the aged. One could say that mental health demands both and that pathology lies in the refusal to accept this fact.

In part psychology can be seen as an evaluation of one's anatomy and physiology. It is based on the ability of human beings to perceive themselves as objects and to evaluate the qualities and the meaning of these objects. In this perspective women have frequently felt injustice in the specifics of their sex. Women have called menstruation "the curse." They have also felt heterosexual union as an experience of invasion which, although potentially pleasurable and fulfilling, is likely to be associated with a violation of one's bodily territory and sometimes with the sense of damage which we usually experience when an object from the outside breaks our bodily boundaries. Certainly in comparison with the male's contribution to reproduction, pregnancy seems to be an overwhelming burden as the female organism becomes increasingly uncomfortable and anxious as the time of delivery approaches. For women who have remained childless or who have lost children, menopause terminates the hope of fulfilling their reproductive potential. Over and beyond that it is a dramatic ending of a body function which has been a monthly experience. It is a precursor of death or at least an indication that other functions are likely to diminish or stop. At any rate, it is a decisive reminder of mortality, although it may also bring relief from both the fears of pregnancy and the discomfort of menstruation. Like all organic events, it is characterized by the potential of enjoyment as well as of discomfort. The specifics of the male body also have their psychological concomitants. Genital functioning holds the potential of power as well as of powerlessness. Failure to prevent an erection and inability to have one in relation to a beloved person both have the connotation of lack of control where control is desired. Being generally expected to have greater muscular strength and height than women, men who lack these attributes may find these deficiences to be a source of dissatisfaction with self and a narcissistic wound to their self-image and sometimes an embarrassment in interaction with women. Male physiology requires confidence and courage in sexual encounters. Failure to respond may lead many men to envy women their power of concealment. Envy, however, is the result of an unpleasant evaluation of oneself as well as a cause of resenting its object.

Traditional male anger is silent anger. It expresses itself in social unresponsiveness, impotence, and lack of attention. It is probably increased by the tendency of most women not to relinquish a maternal stance even where they claim equality with males. A maternal attitude in women who lead socially restricted lives may be more tolerable to men than that shown by women who claim equality. It is easier to be treated as a child by a wife who is a homemaker than to be so treated by a wife who is a competent provider of income. The fact is that men, from infancy on, have been trained to expect happiness from women. It is one of the permanent coping problems of men to find this source of expected happiness to be also a source of irritation.

Psychoanalytic concepts such as the repetition compulsion, the desire for punishment, the incorporation of the aggressor, restriction of the ego and, foremost, the concept of developmental arrest represent a theory of learning in which earlier learning makes later learning difficult. If an infant has learned too well that crying produces the comforting mother, when a two year old has found that only cleanliness secures maternal love, when the "spoiled" child has learned that nobody is so important as oneself and that others can be disregarded or exploited, we have phenomena of mislearning. This makes later learning difficult if not impossible and drives people into therapy to learn there what other people learn in normal development—or to find solace for their inability to learn new coping mechanisms with the challenges of life. These developmental mishaps and the resulting disabilities, however, are only exaggerations of what occurs in all of us. The infant fights the child, the child fights the adolescent, the adolescent fights the adult, the adult the senescent, and the senescent the dying. Development represents therefore a never-ending struggle between old learning and new learning, the demand of giving up old learning and replacing it with new learning while being under permanent risk of falling back upon earlier modes of coping and interaction when the stresses of life become overwhelming. Faced with the difficulties of one's chronological age, the tendency of the human being is to regress toward an earlier stage. This is experienced in all three families through which a human being must find his way during the course of the life cycle. The child must become parent and the parent must become child in the sense of receiving care again. Even if everything one did as a child was adaptive, it becomes maladaptive when one is no longer a child. We permanently outgrow our adaptations.

Another area of familial difficulties is elucidated by psychoanalysis as the attachments of symbolic meaning to people who should have different meanings in one's life. People are not used or treated for what they are but for what they represent to the perceiver. Husbands are used as fathers, wives as mothers and, worse, sometimes children are used as parents. Aging fathers and mothers are sometimes remembered as irritants or even enemies of development with whom one can now get even by treating them as children. Needless to say, it is a permanent temptation and sometimes a rewarding one for spouses to treat one another as children, which might be adaptive particularly in periods of stress, illness, or crisis. It is exceedingly difficult to be adult all the time, but it is maladaptive and frequently intolerable to be treated as a child or as a parent as a permanent condition.

Anatomical and physiological differences, as well as developmental challenges, however, do not complete the range of human experience. Social expectations, traditionally attached to age and sex, and our reactions to them, vastly add to the complexity of living. The vehemence of current public debate and the awareness of rapid social change, particularly in the roles formerly assigned to one or the other gender, force many people today into a decision-making process as to whether they should assume the roles which they believe are expected of them or the roles which they would like to perform. Families may frequently expect a daughter to marry and have children, while the daughter may prefer singlehood and a professional career. She may also be influenced by the message of the Women's Movement and feel that she must have a career although her inclination is to seek the traditional shelter of marriage and the relatively autonomous role of parent. Similarly, males may feel that they have to share domestic tasks with their wives although they do not want to, or they may be ashamed of finding enjoyment in doing it. What has to be considered is that today people are not only role performers but are forced into becoming role selectors. This forces upon almost every young person the task of decision making between two conflicting role-demands: the role demands coming from the outside world, however rightly or wrongly perceived, and the internal role demands that are often in contradiction to the former.

Ideally in a modern marriage it should make no difference who washes the dishes, who diapers the baby, who makes more money in the labor market, since the relationship requires that each do what he or she can to make the other feel stronger. In reality, however, the acceptance of new roles may make one partner of the marital union feel weaker than he or she would feel if such role demands were not perceived as becoming mandatory. Obsolete self-images of what is right for one's sex may interfere with the awareness of social change and the acceptance of exchangeability of roles. The much used term "role negotiation" suggests that in many young marriages the partners try to tell each other that roles which they feel they should assume in daily life make them weaker rather than stronger. This communication also implies that by the performance of these roles they cannot help one another because their resentment or ambivalence makes the undesired role performance ineffective.

What should be faced is the fact that partners in a marital relationship cannot attain self-realization through the role assignments which somehow have come their way simply on the basis of sex or, conceivably, the demands of the relationship. If self-realization is then sought in an attempt to change the maladaptive roles that have been traditionally imposed and in compliance have been attempted, there is likely to be a period of discovery which was not possible while the conflict was unresolved. Any attempt at self-realization is under the threat of becoming routine. Once it becomes routine it ceases to justify the effort that was put into it when it was begun. Only when it proves to have authentic meaning beyond the mere fact of the performance can it really be called a conflict resolution in terms of success. Ultimately, people will have to reformulate the term of self-realization and call it self-proof. Once self-realization has become "only a job" there is no more self-realization. We frequently feel the need to question the assumption that self-realization means a higher degree of satisfaction than renunciation. Self-realization can go both ways. It can turn out negatively. It was the wisdom of Jung not to predict a positive outcome of analysis but to suggest that the result of analysis could be either improvement or a deterioration, an enhancement or a destruction of life. Actually, we have not the slightest reason to assume that a woman will be happier in the office where she is under supervision, with the risk of unemployment, with the pressure of competition not only with men but with other women when the male dominance in employment disappears. Once the experience that was formerly denied has become available and is tested, it may be found by some that being at home and minding the children and being relatively autonomous in these two areas is more agreeable than fighting for survival in the jungle of employment. In the assumption of new roles the role choice is ultimately subject to the test of authenticity. If, after having been tried, a role is found to give the individual a feeling of rightness in the world, then the role choice or role renegotiation has been a success. If it gives the individual a feeling of unsuccessful experimentation and new disappointments, the search for authenticity will have to continue.

We do not wish to suggest, however, that developmental hazards and failures represent the essence of familial experience. They are only the identification of pain and difficulty from which people in a familial context derive their awareness, their potential for satisfying one another, helping one another through growth and development, giving comfort to one another, and ultimately permitting one another—and themselves—to die.

We would like to stress still another perspective, the mutuality of difficulties and rewards in familial interaction. Since human beings need one another, all human interaction must be based on some degree of understanding the needs of the people involved so that they can engage in strengthening exchanges. Communication of these needs, however, is always incomplete. This is so, first of all, because infantile wishes for sensual gratification are buried in the unconscious and return, if they do, only in masked form which prevents us from knowing always what we really want. Secondly, we are frequently reticent in expressing fully what we do know and, ultimately, we are frequently ambivalent about our wish to give and our wish to receive. Interaction, although necessary, is therefore always at risk of being unsatisfactory. Even when developed to a high degree of satisfaction, it is at risk of becoming unsatisfactory again because the persons involved change biologically, physiologically, and psychologically, and will also be affected by changes in their circumstances. Then a new series of experimentation in interaction must be started.

Furthermore, dyadic experiences—the interaction between two persons—have effects upon others. Marital conflict will affect the children. Difficulties between siblings will affect their parents or other siblings. A satisfactory sex life between the spouses may protect the development of their sons and daughters from the risk of being interrupted or disturbed by emotional demands from the parents for compensatory satisfaction.

Every phase of life presents new dyadic challenges, which, if not met, can prevent one from forming other ties in family life. Many people go through life in search of a "good mother," because they did not have one or felt they did not have one when they were children. Such a search can prevent one from forming satisfactory marital relationships because few spouses can substitute for a good mother, and as mentioned above, it is questionable whether they should if they could. Furthermore, a dyadic tie will go frequently through stages of initial disappointment, increasing satisfaction, and then the experience of loss, be it gradual or abrupt. Some interactions remain unsatisfactory; some almost immediately seem to work out and be stable for a long time.

Interactional experiences imply assuming risk-taking responsibilities for others, conquering difficulties through change, and accepting the restlessness of the human condition. Repeatedly focused on these challenges throughout the life cycle, family life is the test of man's humanity to man and, as such, requires optimism and courage. In the end, however, familial life can produce an accumulation of fatigue as a result of meeting challenge after challenge, or despair over having failed to meet the challenges. It can thus prepare one for the acceptance and sometimes for the embracing of death as relief from the pain of separations which cannot be expected to be followed by "new" unions.

SUGGESTED READINGS

Marie Bonaparte, *Female Sexuality*. New York, International Universities Press, 1963.

Erik H. Erikson, *Childhood and Society*. New York, W. W. Norton, 1950.

Sigmund Freud, *Three Essays on the Theory of Sexuality*. New York, Basic Books, 1963.

Warren J. Gadpaille, M.D., *The Cycles of Sex*. Lucy Freeman, ed., New York, Charles Scribner's Sons, 1975.

Martin Heidegger, *Existence and Being* with an introduction and analysis by Werner Brock, Chicago, A Gateway Edition, Henry Regnery, 1949.

William H. Masters, M.D. and Virginia Johnson, *Human Sexual Response*. Boston, Little, Brown and Company, 1966.

————, *Human Sexual Inadequacy*. Boston, Little, Brown and Company, 1970.

Psychoanalysis and Women. Edited by Jean Baker Miller, M.D., New York, Brunner/Mazel Publishers, 1973.

Benjamin J. Sadoch et al., *The Sexual Experience*. Baltimore, Maryland, William and Wilkins, 1976.

Letha Scanzoni and John Scanzoni, *Men, Women, and Change*. New York, McGraw-Hill, 1976.

Separation—Individuation. Essays in Honor of Margaret S. Mahler, John B. McDevitt and Calvin Settlage, eds., New York, International Universities Press, 1971.

Evelyne Sullerot, *Woman, Society and Change*. New York, World University Library, McGraw-Hill, 1971

CHAPTER 2

Family Discomforts:
Irritation or Pathology

There is a tendency in our society to equate family discomforts with pathology and to suggest that such discomforts can be removed only by the intervention of psychiatrists, clinical psychologists, sex therapists, child guidance workers, therapeutic camps, encounter groups, etc. Every year witnesses the appearance of new catagories of professionals that claim competence and legitimacy in treating family discomforts and diseases. We deplore this tendency and consider the bipolarity between comfort and discomfort as an essential connection of family life which repeats itself through all phases of development. It seems important, therefore, to offer from the start a distinction between the irritations of family life and pathology. We will try to show that irritation is unavoidable and does not necessarily indicate the presence of pathology. In various ways irritation is a challenge to growth or to an acceptance of the situation, which is also a form of growth because it at least releases energy for other areas of development.

It seems to us that the irritation in family life starts with irritation with self. Developmentally speaking, an infant is undoubtedly irritated with himself because of the helplessness, dependency, and discomfort that his physiological stage involves. One need only visualize an infant lying in his crib, crying and making futile efforts to change his position, to know that inherent in the human body is a negative evaluation of the body's limitations. This is true at the beginning of life and at an advanced age. The senile person must experience frustrations similar to those of the infant. We need only think of the stroke patient who has to wait for the nurse to turn him and of the bedsores that he suffers if he is not turned often enough. For aging people the experience of losing hearing or, at least of losing the power of discrimination among sounds, and the appearance of double vision after a period of reading are other causes of irritation with the failing of their bodies.

Physiological inadequacy is always experienced as an irritant to self. We suggest that irritations are, at their root, negative evaluations of a lack of autonomy in changing one's existence to a higher level of functioning or of restoring oneself to a level of functioning once possessed. In the stages between infancy and senescence there are irritations with development similar in kind, if not in intensity. The child experiences limiting care, such as restriction of movement in space and playtime activity or structuring of sleeping time, as irritations. Curfews set for adolescents are social limitations which need not be imposed in an authoritarian way to present a source of discomfort. When parents worry about adolescents, they produce an irritant which the adolescent cannot remove because of his still partial dependence on his parents and also because of his love for them or, at least, of ambivalence toward them. The whole experience of singlehood which tends to occupy larger and larger stretches of developmental time involves and implies irritation with self. It lacks the experience of wholeness which can be derived from a union such as marriage provides. Not to be cared for by others when needed is an irritation frequently experienced in this life style. Loneliness is sometimes a high price to pay for autonomy. It may lead some people to seek in therapy what others find in family life, predictable human contact and empathy.

We therefore enter family life, whether in the parent-child relationship, the marital relationship, or the aging-parent/adult-son-or-daughter relationship, with considerable irritation with self, but there are also other irritations. In the encounter with a person of the other sex in marriage or even in quasi marital arrangements between persons of the same sex, we may have the genetically determined irritants of having been born with different congenital behavior patterns. Some are born to be slow, some are born to be fast. In order to live together, the faster one has to slow down or the slower one has to rush. Usually the convoy principle will prevail and living together will mean slowing down to accommodate the slower person—obviously at the price of irritating the faster one. In the less frequent cases of rushing through life with a congenitally fast person, it is obvious that there will be irritation caused by the breathless pace.

Another type of irritation which probably enters family life occurs in the selection of a marriage partner. It happens frequently that one of the spouses has decided on the marriage earlier than the other and that the one who has to wait usually enters the marriage with a considerable backlog of irritation. One could almost say that the experience of living from infancy to the stage of one's marriage is one of accumulating layer upon layer of irritation, which must be dealt with by one's spouse at the same time his or her own irritations require reciprocal coping.

People frequently enter into marriage with the silent but determined decision to change their partners in one respect or other. When attempts at change are then made, however lovingly, they are an insult to the individual's development at the stage to which it has progressed because the implication is that one is not good enough as one is and that the other has the power to impose change. Such implications of inferiority and superiority are probably the most frequent irritations of marital life. Development is made possible essentially by optimism about its results: limitations will become smaller and adaptations more effective and, in one's fantasy, lasting. Such optimism is permanently under attack if one's marriage partner suggests that what has been achieved so far is not enough or unfortunate. Ultimately, it means that one's development is taken over by husband or wife and that one is deprived of autonomy in this essential life experience. Where such interactions of attempted alterations persist, the irritation frequently becomes intolerable because hope is lost that it will come to an end. Such a situation implies that one or the other will not be permitted to live as an adult, and irritation is very likely to change into hatred.

At this point in our discussion we are verging on problems of pathology. As previously stated, we do not plan to present a description of family pathologies or of family therapies. Our concern is to deal with universals which distinguish unavoidable irritations from pathology. The essential criterion of difference, we think, lies in the dimension of time: irritations which are intermittent, which come to an end, or are inter-spaced by periods of harmony belong to the range of the normal. Irritations which do not stop have the implication that something is seriously wrong and therefore cannot be considered as normal. When family members do not make up after having annoyed one another, when children don't forgive their parents and parents don't forgive their children, negative feelings and hopelessness combine to create a condition of total stagnation in family life—a condition which is pathological because it interrupts development and kills the hope for development. Family pathology in our view can therefore be called "irritation without self-repair." In this case we refer to "the self" not of the individual family members but of the totality of the family membership. This is an essential point because in a given family it takes at least two persons if not more to cause family pathology; in our view, it is erroneous to think that a single person can make an entire family sick, since the family is a web of interactions.

An example of the pathological network of family relationships might be a bad marriage in which the wife constantly nags her husband about what he should do, about what the children should not do and what he should do to make the children stop doing what they do. Another example is a family situation in which the husband withdraws into hostile silence. The husband feels that his wife's nagging makes family life intolerable. The wife feels that the husband's unresponsiveness forces her into the nagging. She thinks that if he would talk, she would not have to nag. He thinks that if she would not nag, he could talk. The reality of the situation is that the behavior of one is provoking the behavior of the other and vice versa.

It is probably a universal experience in the parent-child relationship that parents want their children to change and children want their parents to change. Where these conditions become long-lasting, there is family pathology because the continuation of discomfort has a malignant effect on development or at least will stop development at a specific stage. Such situations can be repaired only through therapy or separation. Where neither occurs, family pathology will become permanent and will entirely lose the bipolarity of comfort and discomfort. It will turn into a living hell in which people feel both separated and confined. One cannot help but think of a cell block in which prisoners are incarcerated, forced into togetherness but separated by metal bars from one another.

Another frequent characteristic of family pathology is the waiting of one family member for the other or others to take the initiative in bringing about improvement. This implies a judgmental stance, which is erroneous because as indicated above, there is never only one person who has to change in a pathological relationship. It is also likely to be nonproductive because it may make the other person or persons assume the same stance of waiting for the initiative to be taken by someone else. It produces stagnant reciprocity of pathology. This waiting for others to change is actually a show of power. It means, "I will make you change without having to change myself," or "I will change only if you do."

It also happens that on occasion one family member masochistically assumes the total guilt of having caused chronic family discomfort. The assumption of such a stance can either be an unconscious plea for forgiveness, or for reassurance that one is really not the cause of the trouble. It is anything but an assessment of the true situation.

We will frequently refer to the key concepts of transactional analysis, namely, of treating an adult person as a child and of treating a child as an adult person or, in other words, to the "parenting" of spouses and the "spousing" of children. When such treatments become permanent, family pathology probably displays one of its clearest expressions and consequences: the interruption of development.

Something which is not sufficiently mentioned, although it happens with great frequency, is family pathology based on structural deficits or surpluses. Family pathology must result when there are so many members in a family that none can receive a sufficient measure of attention, care, and response. A mother with eleven children will find it difficult, if not impossible, to be a good mother. She will probably feel that she cannot be a good mother, will become angry with herself, with her children, and with her destiny, and will become even worse than her situation would understandably force her to be. Such situations occur mostly in disadvantaged population groups who either do not use birth control because they are not aware of it or because they do not care.

In advantaged population groups we also have similar problems as a result of many divorces which do not lead to remarriages. Here we have single parents who suffer from overload. The single parent, usually the mother, will assume the role of both parents and will have to be provider and nurturer and ideally, should be on the lookout for a new spouse. She will, therefore, have to carry the burdens of singlehood, will have to protect herself emotionally against spousing her children and will simply have to carry a family without sufficient personnel to help her. Since all overloads, however bravely carried, lead to exhaustion, and since exhaustion leads either to rage or depression, single-parent families are likely to present family pathology, particularly if no effort is being made to restore the family personnel by a remarriage.

We would like to conclude this chapter with the suggestion of a "do it yourself test" regarding family health. If irritation and discomfort have existed in your family, ask yourself whether you are willing and able to change the way you have been behaving. If you come to the conclusion that you cannot or do not want to change, you probably are part of a pathological family constellation.

SUGGESTED READINGS

Henry D. Aiken, *Reason and Conduct*. New York, Knopf, 1963.
John Bowlby, *Attachment and Loss*. New York, Basic Books, 1969.
H. V. Dichs, *Marital Tensions*. New York, Basic Books, 1967.
The Family in Contemporary Society. Iago Galdston, ed., New York, International Universities Press, 1958.

Anna Freud, *Normality and Pathology in Childhood.* New York, International Universities Press, 1965.

Erich Fromm, *The Sane Society.* New York, Holt, Rinehart & Co., 1960.

Irving D. Harris, *Normal Children and Mothers.* Glencoe, Ill., Free Press of Glencoe, 1959.

Marie Jahoda, *Current Concepts of Positive Mental Health.* New York, Basic Books, 1959.

Melanie Klein, *Contributions to Psychoanalysis.* London, Hogarth Press, 1948.

Daniel Offer and Melvin Sabshin, *Normality.* New York, Basic Books, 1966.

Virginia Satir, *Conjoint Family Therapy.* Palo Alto, California, Science and Behavior Books, 1967.

H. Stierlin, *Conflict and Reconciliation.* Garden City, N. Y., Doubleday, Anchor Books, 1969.

Part II

Relationship Experiences
in Childhood

CHAPTER 3

Primary Experiences:
The Infant Experiences
Himself and His Mother

In the strictest sense of the term, a "report" on how the infant experiences himself and his mother could be written only by people who remember their own infancy, how they saw themselves at that stage of life, how they began to separate themselves from the whole world and experienced this new separate world in terms of the person who gave them sustenance, nurture, and a symbiotic experience approaching the physical union which was lost at birth. In the perspective of history, that person was not always the biological mother. It could have been a wet nurse, and in modern times it could be the father or an employee in an infant day care center. The use of the term "mother" as a generic term for all these persons seems appropriate, however, because the biological tie between the infant and his mother makes her particularly committed to this task and will probably do so in the future.

The large and significant amount of knowledge which is believed to exist regarding infant development and the mother-infant relationship was gathered by those researchers who, like us, faced the obstacle of childhood amnesia and therefore were deprived of the echo of experience which provides the ultimate basis for an acceptance of research findings. Whatever we were told about our infancy and the first two years of life is the report of observations made about us by others. It was largely the work of Freud's daughter, Anna, as well as that of Melanie Klein, which through interpreting the behavior and particularly the play of children started to identify the fund of accumulated but unconscious experiences with which a child starts consciousness. There is a certain drama in the fact that we enter the world of recall with a backlog and burden of experiences to which we have no direct access for the rest of our lives. We can only hypothesize what we experienced as infants and validate our hypotheses by observations of other infants. More important, what a mother thinks her infant child experiences is also the only basis on which she can operate. Such thinking, however, is assumption and not information.

With this reservation, we venture to say that the sensitivity of the mother to changes in their well-being is the essential experience of the newborn. Even if they were not by their early stage of maturation and by their limitations of perception unable to think in terms other than those related to themselves, their vulnerability would force them to be egotists from the start. This egotistical stance toward the world is only slowly and ambivalently given up in the course of maturation and development, and only the advancing years make it possible for us to transcend it. One could therefore say that all human beings start as egotists and, if they attain wisdom, can end as altruists. Of course, some of us die too soon or too late and some of us die without this attainment; the baseline of egotism in the human experience however is always there and must be kept in mind in the discussion of all stages of development. We assume that infants live in a totally egotistical world in which they experience their surroundings, human or otherwise, merely as extensions of themselves. This experience is not only perceptual and does not mean that they are not aware of their body boundaries. It is also globally evaluative insofar as infants cannot yet distinguish between themselves and others as a source of pain and relief. Being fed, cleaned, soothed, burped, cradled and sometimes catered to or not catered to emerge only gradually as forms of interaction between the infant and others, and they are always evaluated in terms of tension reduction and a feeling of well-being for the infant.

This process is frequently complicated by difficulties in communication. Basically, communication between infants and mothers is not speech communication but body communication. Probably the first communication experienced is being held tightly by an adult. The next would be the communication of exchange: the infant is hungry or uncomfortable and gets fed and signs of satisfaction such as quieting down are the rewards of the mother.

As an adult who has learned to separate herself from the universe as an individual and to interact symbolically with other individuals, the mother of the newborn is faced with the task of interacting and of understanding someone who is not a symbolic interactor. The infant has no or only a limited command of words which makes action necessary for the conveying of meaning. This is the basic difficulty in communication between child and mother. It is one of the basic anxieties of mothers who have borne their first child that they will not understand what the child needs, that they will not be able to interpret the child's repertoire of expression, and that, as a result, the child will fail to thrive. The infant's cry is a universal sign of discomfort, but this limited form of communication is non-specific and the mother can only guess at the problem requiring a remedy. The assumption may be simply that the infant is hungry or feels pain. It is possible, however, that the crying is related to discomfort in a specific part of the body which is not manifested in an external change. The mother is therefore not always able to assess the seriousness of the infant's complaint and to provide appropriate relief. In simple terms, how does one give a specific response to a non-specific stimulus? A similar problem is faced by an active mother who has a placid baby. She may be afraid, without reason, that the child is retarded. On the other hand, a placid mother may find herself irritated by an active baby.

The situation is aggravated because, in modern circumstances, there are few experienced women of an earlier generation who, as part of the household, could tell the new mother on the basis of their own experiences what the crying of an infant is likely to mean. At the same time the responsibility for infant care has become highly personal and focused on the mother. She is held responsible not only for her children's well-being, but also for their mental health corresponding to their stages of development, such as acquiring trust in the first year of life.

Thus, infants have unavoidably the experience of being misunderstood, of being limited by inability to move their bodies without help, of receiving care which often brings no relief and of being exposed to the repetitive sequence of discomfort and comfort. The infant situation is comparable to the helplessness of the mute or the paralyzed individual who is dependent for relief on the good fortune of having an experienced and skillful caretaker. Infants, therefore, take "potluck" with their mothers, but even the lucky ones will have a sufficient amount of frustration to grow up with a residue of resentment. Even they, equipped with a measure of trust which they gained in interaction with an adequate mother, will be found unequipped to cope with the enormity of unexpected upheavals and tragedies.

On the other hand, those infants who survive a large measure of inadequate care and nurture will retain a minimum of optimism that discomfort and misfortune do not kill. Thus, all infants experience one of the greatest problems of human existence, namely, the inconsistency and unreliability of human relations in terms of satisfying one's needs. Infancy is the baseline for two universal experiences: the feeling of not being understood and the apprehension or even surprise that nobody can be relied upon to be always one thing or the other and that the same person can be the source of both pleasure and discomfort. In summary, it is in infancy that the basis is laid for the most difficult learning experience that human beings have to master—that one must go through life without being fully understood, and without fully understanding those for whom one cares or of whom one is afraid.

Considering the odds against survival, such as their overwhelming helplessness, the survival rate of infants in modern times has been dramatically improved. In addition to care provided by mothers, parents, spouses, or older siblings, there is now the support system involving hospitals, day care centers, public health nurses, and baby clinics which increases the chances for survival of children born into our society.

The next phase of the infant's experience could probably best be described as differentiation and egotism emerging from confusion. Although the child is born with only one organ ready for functional contact with the world, his mouth, and otherwise is completely at the mercy of others, infancy is an experience of dramatic maturation and development. The child discovers the breasts of his mother, his own body, then the total mother or the total child-care person and, perhaps most important, the phenomenon of having others turn their faces and bodies toward him. The message of the turning toward the infant means, of course, that he or she is important; it affirms the infant as relevant. The infant begins to expect comfort from posturing that signifies approach. He or she learns the simple responses, i.e., to interpret the smile of someone approaching as a signal of impending gratification to which one responds with the facial acknowledgment of anticipatory pleasure, a smile. Most of all, there is an increasing intensity in the infant's awareness of mother as the essential person in his or her life. With the understanding that the mother is more than just another adult begins the rejection of people other than the mother. The smiling response becomes confined to the mother, discrimination sets in, and children discover the function of turning away. They show the essential grasp of the fact that if one doesn't want to interact, one must turn away from a person who turns toward one. Everyone who has seen infants, still helpless in body movement and forced to lie on their backs, turn their heads to one or the other side when somebody approaches may become aware of the fact that, even in infancy, the human being discovers that some elements of dyadic relationships are good and that others are not.

The symbiotic relationship is the first attempt during the course of one's life to overcome the physical separation which occurs at birth. It is an experiential learning of reunification to be put to a mother's breast, to be cradled, to identify the smell of another's body and to derive comfort from it. The child has learned to expect comfort, that food means love and that bodily comfort can be expected from closeness, specifically from the mother, i.e., the psychological meaning of physical experience. The mother has learned better to understand the signals of the child; she is beginning to learn a new language, baby talk. Child and mother have emerged victorious from the tribulations of coping with lack of understanding and difficulties in communication.

SUGGESTED READINGS

S. Brady, *Patterns of Mothering.* New York, International Universities Press, 1956.

W. R. D. Fairbairn, *Psychoanalytic Studies of the Personality.* London, Tavistock, 1952.

Melanie Klein, *The Psychoanalysis of Children.* London, Hogarth Press, 1932.

Parenthood. Its Psychology and Psychopathology. E. James Anthony and Therese Benedek, eds., Boston, Little, Brown and Company, 1970

M. Ribble, *The Rights of Infants.* New York, Columbia University Press, 1943.

René A. Spitz, *The First Year of Life.* New York, International Universities Press, 1965.

D. W. Winnicott, *The Maturational Processes and the Facilitating Environment.* London, Hogarth Press, 1965.

The Writings of Anna Freud. New York, International Universities Press, 1968.

CHAPTER 4

Multiple Relationships and Heterosexuality: Children Experience Their Parents

Most children lose the relative simplicity of early infancy through the discovery that mother is beginning to make demands and that there are more people of relevance in the world than they themselves and their mothers.

Parents experience in their relationship to their children in their second year of life a struggle for power which expresses itself frequently in the mundane problem of toilet training. According to Erikson's widely accepted developmental schema, the world meets children in the years of life before school around those parts of their body which have matured into functioning. Infants' needs are met around concern for intake, their mouth, two year olds who can sit up are trained to control elimination, and children who have developed the ability to walk are being restricted from going where they want to, such as crossing streets against traffic, entering the bedroom of their parents when the latter wish privacy, etc.

The obsessive cleanliness of Western middle class people makes children a domestic discomfort until they have obtained bowel control and exercise it according to the expectation of parents and child-care workers. In this fight, will of the child is pitted against will of the adult, and since the physical superiority of the parent makes this a very unequal battle, it provides for many mothers an experience of power which in our democratic society they would probably be horrified to admit. In this context, it has been observed that women are less squeamish about cleaning children and administering bowel training than are men. It has been suggested, however, to one of the authors by a female teaching associate that this relative lack of disgust of women for the feces of children is confined to their own children and that the vomit and feces of other children are just as repulsive to them as feces and vomit generally are to men.

It has been proposed in psychoanalytic literature that some people derive such meaning from their toilet-training experiences in this period of life that withholding, hoarding, and being punctilious and conscientious become part of their permanent character structure. Fantastic as this may sound, such people make trustworthy adults, people on whom one can rely, good citizens— and, conceivably, people with sadomasochistic fantasies in their sexual predilections. Again on the negative side, it may be pointed out that parents who fail to achieve control over their children in this period of life may experience a feeling of powerlessness and inadequacy. From the children's point of view, this may result in such unhappy consequences for their development as resentment and a feeling that they are unloved and therefore unlovable. As a byproduct of group living in which numbers of couples now try to escape the chores and boredom of traditional middle class house-keeping, toilet training becomes much less important. The environment of the children is generally so untidy that being messy does not become a battle issue between parents and children with conceivably undesirable developmental outcome. The same is true, of course, for people who for reasons of poverty have to crowd children and adults into inadequate space.

Equally important to the struggle for power and autonomy is the orientation to a home in which there are fathers, brothers, sisters, and possibly other relatives, particularly in such families where grandparents share the household. In certain modern arrangements where there are two women living together the child may be faced with "father" figures who are women. Whatever the complexities of the household membership in which the children discover that there are more people than they originally perceived, they must learn to cope with problems of rejection. They may have to learn that they must turn away from their mother if they want to turn toward father, that their mother turns away from them and turns toward other children or toward her husband. They may learn that grandmothers turn to them and mothers don't. They are faced with the task of coping with multiple relationships. Since our bodies are so built that we can face and turn toward only one other person at a time, every multiple relationship carries the possibility of rejection or being rejected. Since rejection is experienced by the person rejected as an unfriendly act or a threat, the child learns the bipolarity of this physiologically determined necessity. Where there are more than two persons, one cannot turn toward somebody without turning away from somebody else, who is unlikely to respond positively to this rejection. Children, and particularly first children, are very sensitive in this respect. They cannot welcome the arrival of a sibling. They cannot be pleased when mother or father or caretaker turns away from them in order to turn to somebody else. They feel temporarily abandoned and will be angry, jealous, or feel threatened. There are, however, comforting experiences when people who have turned away from them come back and turn toward them and they learn to reciprocate.

No matter how much fathers may try to share the nurturing tasks with their wives, no matter how much child-care workers may take over the functions for certain periods of the day, the relationship between a child and a mother remains symbiotic to a degree beyond the first year of life since both share life in a unique way. Male or female, a child *is* his or her mother biologically. Even after birth, when separation takes place, the child remains biologically a part of the mother. This unity is strengthened through the routine of care and the extensive amount of time during which they are together day after day. Of course, even biological mothers can be ambivalent about their children, but the positive side of the ambivalence seems to be stronger and more frequent.

As in all other discussions in this book, we are trying here to widen the range of normality. We know that there are rejecting mothers and we know that there are doting fathers, but we do believe that health represents a broad stretch of human experience bordered by narrow bands of pathology in either direction.

Since the children are not borne by the father, they must learn to know him in the sense of establishing a relationship with a stranger. The father is often connected in the child's experience only with a release from routine because he is usually not around when the routine of a child's life takes place. In former times he may have been a disciplinarian, but today he tends more and more to be a buddy or a friend. Only slowly is social change allowing some fathers the chance to have close contact with their children during times other than merely evenings and weekends and to assume the role of caretaker and nurturer.

The symbiotic relationship with the mother and the deepening "acquaintance" relationship with the father provide children with the complementary aspects of parental experience. A sufficient relationship with both father and mother will enable the child to handle closeness as well as distance in human relationships and to experience both as challenges to mastery rather than as threats to existence. Even where parents disagree on child rearing and disapprove of each other's performance as a parent, there may be an important developmental lesson for children. One may be disapproved of by one but approved of by another.

Over and beyond closeness and distance, approval and disapproval, the child has to learn from the parents sex-specific and sex-responsive behavior. This is true also in our times of exchangeable roles and occurs frequently on an unconscious level. In the son's experience the father guides and advises him in learning to cope with man's traditional responsibilities, which essentially require aggressive and acquisitive qualities and mechanical skills. His mother generally emphasizes in the training of her son—frequently unconsciously—the traditionally more feminine concerns with self-maintenance, protectiveness toward others and tenderness. In the girl's experience the mother provides a female behavior model. Even if a mother is liberated and does what was once traditionally man's work, she still cannot help conveying the role model of motherhood to the child because this is a biological and psychological experience that cannot be eradicated by emphasizing the exchangeability of sex roles in social and economic areas. Still the father cannot help conveying unconsciously a male role model because he cannot prevent in a good relationship at least partial identification with him—a male. We have, therefore at least in our culture, child rearing conditions which result in the likelihood that all persons carry within themselves the bipolar tendencies of masculinity and feminity, although conceivably males will find it easier to express the masculine elements because they have been reinforced through societal influences. Similarly, and for the same reasons, females will find it easier to express the female elements in their personality make-up.

Under the impact of social change it is likely that repression, or at least suppression, of these bipolar tendencies will not find as much social support as in the past. This may lead either to conflict and conscious ambivalence or, in more fortunate cases of development, to a wider and more harmonious combination of male and female traits in the male. The development may be enhanced by the employment of male workers in day care centers and nursery schools and by a return of men to elementary school teaching.

Of course, there are children who are reared without fathers and in the future there may be more and more children who are reared without mothers, but in all likelihood these will be exceptions to the rule. This bipolar orientation should also be welcomed because, in a society of exchangeable roles, males will have to draw on their incorporated feminity and females on their incorporated masculinity in order to perform these roles adequately and in a relatively conflict-free way. We may never reach familiarity with the physiological and anatomical specifics of the other sex but we may be able to reach familiarity with the psychological derivatives of these specificities. We may be able to incorporate them into our personality set-up and thereby be able to live better with our irreducible differences. To give one particular example of the desirability of this orientation, with more and more people continuing to live beyond seventy, it may become important for husbands to extend nurture, not only to their children but also to their spouses, to feel tenderness for weakness and to regard services resulting from such tenderness as ego-enhancing rather than demeaning. Similarly, the aggressive or resourceful female may well become appreciated as the source of economic support not only for her children but for her husband rather than being regarded as a "misleading" role model for her daughters.

If we remain sex-specific, we find the advantage of identity derived from difference, and if we find familiarity in a person of the other sex, we find the maintaining and life-reproducing function of hererosexual attraction. In the past our social structure has traditionally favored only the first function of parent-child interaction, namely, that of sexual identification. Now we are beginning to experiment with deemphasizing this difference-enhancing tendency and are trying to reinforce the familiar in the difference; in other words, the universals in difference.

The interplay between both these tendencies gives our children a bisexual orientation, not in the sense of sexual variance, such as homosexuality or lesbianism, but in the sense of being better equipped to understand themselves and other members of their own sex as well as members of the opposite sex. In the foreseeable future all children will be exposed to the affective capacities of the mother as well as the coping abilities of the father and be able to integrate these influences without societal opposition. One could go even further and say that in many instances they will be exposed to the coping capabilities of their mothers and the affective capacities of the father without having to hide the personality characteristics derived from such experiences. The encounter with both parents will lead to one of the most essential experiences of heterosexual compatibility. Modern child care facilities will probably have male as well as female personnel and so will have the school system. Male and female behavior models are likely therefore to enter the developmental experience of most children.

In the period between three and five years of age, children enjoy their newly gained power of moving around without the help of adults for intrusive exploration of the environment and encounter, in these ventures, the custodial as well as the private and exclusive concerns of their parents. In their explorations, they will clash against the inhibiting tendencies of parents who want to protect their children from the risk of accidents, from encounter with the primal scene, or from premature stimulation of their sexuality. This is, therefore, a period in which curiosity and adventure are not encouraged. Psychoanalytic terminology refers to this phase of development as the genital stage because of the role that sexual curiosity and stimulation play in it, but the term is too restrictive. Ability of movement and its restrictions involve also other experiences such as exploration of the wider environment and escape from confining safeguards.

Adding still more difficulty to this stage of development is a pronounced tendency of children to reach out sensually and emotionally toward the parent of the other sex. This relationship approach is usually designated as the oedipal phase, and it is largely discussed in terms of the child's experience of rejection and terror of punishment for fantasies in which the parent of the same sex is removed and the parent of the other sex accepts the child as an emotional partner in lieu of his spouse. Where sexual inadequacy seemed to be traceable to such experiences, the older literature of psychoanalysis refers to these as Oedipus complexes. It may be recalled that in Greek mythology, Oedipus unwittingly killed his father and married his mother and when he discovered what he had done, blinded himself as punishment. Less frequently mentioned is the parental reaction to this developmental stage in children. Since most marriages are contracted in an utopian frame of mind but experienced in an atmosphere of realism, an element of disappointment is an inherent part of the marital experience. No marriage partner fully lives up to the desires of the partner and marriage maintenance is frequently bolstered by hopes for later fulfillment or a decision of what one will settle for rather than of what should be demanded. The reaching out of a child toward the parent of the other sex meets, therefore, a certain emotional vulnerability which many people will be able to control but some will not. Where there is parental failure to control positive response to the oedipal reaching out of their children, they may become panicky with the fear of punishment, which they connect with their wish fulfillment. Such children may develop nightmares, may seduce parents into administering corporal punishment, which will serve at the same time to provide a measure of atonement and a measure of sensual gratification through body contact and intimacy with the punishing parent. Similar results may occur where the parents become anxious or even panicky in turn and respond with abrupt rejection.

Even where the parents handle the oedipal reaching out of their children without encouraging response or overdetermined rejection, there remains an unconscious desire in many children which later expresses itself in their choice of a mate similar to the father in the husband or the mother in the wife.

The sense of competition experienced in the oedipal situation

may also be extended to siblings. In that age period, brothers may
be attracted to sisters and sisters to brothers. Sensual attraction
may even operate between children of the same sex. This attraction
may result in a dilution of the oedipal tie to parents. Such a
dilution may actually serve a development-protective function, and
one might speculate whether it is not fortunate if parents do not
perceive sensual elements in the relationship between their children
of preschool age. Even middle-class people may have no awareness
whatsoever of the implications of letting young brothers and sisters
sleep together in the same room and may not worry about the
opportunities of intimate contact created in such situations.
Eventually, however, sleeping arrangements of siblings in most
families will separate the sexes, and opportunities for undetected
sensual and sexual experimentation between them will disappear.

At any rate, oediapal experience on the inter-and intra-
generational level is part of the experience of children before they
go to elementary school. It is a valuable experience because it is a
lesson in which a person must experience defeat in order to develop
adequately, i.e., one learns that feelings of inferiority are by no
means necessarily connected with permanent failure to succeed and
may actually be preconditions of further gains in attaining adequacy and maturity.

Many childhood experiences are those of inferiority, but one
gradually learns that this feeling is likely to diminish and that this
lessening of inferiority as one grows up is really a basis for the
courage to live and to entertain an optimistic view toward the
future. In essence, one learns that time is on one's side.

For many children in both blue- and white-collar population
groups, the child-care burden of the parents is lightened, but also
diluted, by children's services which have been virtually "mother
services." In the developmental schema which we follow in this
book, however, they also have to be examined from the child's
point of view.

Traditionally, the child encountered the school system at age six.
The pioneering of Friedrich Froebel and Maria Montessori helped
to push this encounter back to age five, through the creation of the
kindergarten. Then child-care services were pushed back further to
ages three or four by the establishment of nursery schools. More

recently, day care centers were established for children in the first two years of life.

With public attention focused on the Women's Movement, it is easy to forget that day care centers were originally established to make it possible for mothers to enter factory work. It is a relatively recent development that young middle-class women can be seen dropping their children off on their way to graduate school classes.

Whether or not these various forms of institutional child care are class-oriented or social-progress-oriented, the experience of the child is routine separation from the parents in the morning and return to the family home in the afternoon. In some instances it may be the father who brings the child to the day care center or the nursery school. On an impressionistic basis, the senior author has observed that on arrival at the day care center, children find it easier to separate from their fathers than from their mothers.

Once children are at the day care center or nursery school, they are likely to have the experience of entering a fairy-tale world peopled by youngsters of the same age, with rooms equipped for their capacities. This is a more manageable world than a home world can be. There is also a person in attendance who, for the time he or she is there, has no other function than caring for the children in their group. Mothers may have to divide their time between child care, cooking, cleaning, paying bills, studying, spending time with father, chatting with friends over the telephone. The day care worker is on a job in the children's service with few permissible distractions. The relationship may be more satisfactory than the one the child has with his or her mother, who must also perform family and adult duties other than child care. Still, it is not a dyadic symbiosis but group life with the experience of repetitive rejections that are inherent in multiple relationships.

In essence, what institutional child care injects into a child's life is the phenomenon of repetitive separation from and reunion with the parents on a weekday basis. It implies the experience of an environment which is made much more manageable than a room in the home can provide. It has given the child a children's world. It has given him care by strangers, and thus has exposed him to the risk of loss in cases of labor turnover.

If one sees these experiences in the perspective of the family life cycle, one cannot help but marvel at the preparatory quality of this experience. All familial experiences are a succession of separations and reunions, of feeling accepted and rejected, of wanting to monopolize another person and not being able to.

SUGGESTED READINGS

The Child in his Family. E. James Anthony and Cyrille Koupernik, eds., New York, Wiley-Interscience, 1970

K. Chukovsky, *From Two to Five.* translated and edited by Miriam Morton, Berkeley, University of California Press, 1966.

V. J. Fontana, *The Maltreated Child.* Springfield, Ill. Thomas, 1964.

Selma Fraiberg, *The Magic Years.* New York, Charles Scribner's Sons, 1959.

Sigmund Freud, "On the Sexual Theories of Children," in *The Standard Edition of the Complete Psychological Works of Sigmund Freud.* Vols. 15 and 16, London, Hogarth Press, 1954.

Frank O'Connor, "My Oedipus Complex," in *Stories of Frank O'Connor,* New York, Knopf, 1952.

Jean Piaget, *Play, Dreams, and Imitation in Childhood.* New York, W. W. Norton, 1962.

Beatrice B. Whiting, *Six Cultures: Studies of Child Rearing.* New York, Wiley, 1963.

CHAPTER 5

Biological Auxiliaries: Children Experience their Siblings[1]

It is one of the interesting aspects of modern family sociology, child psychology and child psychiatry that the relationship between brothers and sisters is perceived largely as one of jealousy and discomfort. "Sibling rivalry" is the key concept under which reference to the relationship between brothers and sisters is frequently found in the indexes of textbooks, and even where cooperation among siblings has been perceived by social scientists, they have failed to consider it as significant enough to list it as a concept equivalent to the more negative one. At the same time, a nagging suspicion that the only child is deprived of developmental advantages enjoyed by children who have brothers and sisters has remained active in the minds of parents and research scientist without, however, being either confirmed or disapproved by scientific inquiry.

Strangely enough, American parents, for whom child rearing has become a problem-solving task rather than a natural process, await the birth of a second or third child with the feeling that they are gaining something at the expense of their child or children already born. They feel apprehensive, if not guilty, about the shock

---

[1] The content of this chapter was presented by the senior author at an Institute arranged by Family and Children's Service of Pittsburgh and published by that agency in 1960 in a symposium volume entitled *Understanding Family Dynamics.*

they are going to inflict on their existing offspring and make careful preparations to soften the blow of acquiring a sibling. With their attention thus geared to the perception of discomforts in the sibling relationships between their children, parents are likely to find what they are expecting, namely, sibling rivalry. Every squabble between siblings then becomes confirmation that by having more than one child they have created unhappiness for the older one, if not for the other or others, and that it requires special child-rearing skill to undo or minimize the emotional damage so inflicted.

This strange feeling of guilt over having started a natural and ultimately desirable process has various cultural reasons which bear at least cursory inspection in the context of this chapter. First of all, we have the tendency to claim not only the pursuit but also the possession of happiness as an inalienable right and are inclined to think that absence or interruption of happiness is an indication of failure, if not a pathology. Secondly, the American parent in interaction with the child-rearing professions has developed a great readiness to accept guilt for whatever negative development their children may show. Mothers have become afraid of turning out to be the stereotypical "Moms," and fathers have so abdicated their roles as guides and models for their adolescent children that they have frequently brought upon themselves their contempt. Most important, however, parents have accepted the almost absurd assignment of being responsible not only for their children's physicat maturation, morals and social effectiveness but also for their moods. Thus they have accepted the unrealistic task of rearing their children in a way that would keep them in an almost permanent state of emotional comfort.

Another cultural value which tends to bias and sometimes to block the perception of parents regarding the healthy aspects of sibling relationships is the democratic concept of equality which tends to spill over into the family. It gives parents a feeling of obligation to treat all their children alike and to feel guilty when they find it impossible to respond with equal love to the various personalities represented by their children. In some cases it causes parents to become preoccupied with hopeless attempts to allocate equally among their children all that they have to give. Education must be equally provided, recreation must be equally provided, gifts must be evenly distributed. This tendency toward equality in the treatment of children disregards the essential inequality among children in the family who are normally differentiated from one another by age, sex, intelligence, appearance, and ability to respond warmly to their parents. Disregard of these differences and of their impact upon what a parent can do and feel for a child frequently puts upon the parents an unrealistic emotional burden and thus interferes with their effectiveness in the performance of parental functions.

There is probably no field of social interaction in our society in which disturbance of the peace is viewed with greater concern than the relationship among siblings. It is true that peace is a highly desirable state of affairs (in interpersonal as well as in international affairs). It is considered particularly valuable in a society such as ours where the influence of Christianity is felt in the moral judgment of believers as well as nonbelievers. Unduly and unfortunately, however, it tends to make parents uncomfortable and overly concerned about expressions of sibling rivalry, of fights between brothers and sisters, of quarrels and temporary alienations. Our concern with harmony in the family leads parents to overlook the fact that many quarrels between children are experiments in dealing with conflict, that they provide the basis for experiences in peacemaking, and that they provide a relatively harmless testing ground for skills which must be developed in order to meet the problems of disagreement and conflict in later life.

Over and beyond this cultural pressure which tends to make it difficult for parents to perceive the values of apparently negative interaction between siblings, there are, of course, also expressions of personal difficulties or of personality problems which make parents uncomfortable over familial relationships. There is frequently an unconscious vanity which makes parents feel that they are so precious to their first child that they cannot be shared by him or her with another child. The idea that one is so important to another human being that one cannot give of oneself to anybody else without damaging the former is likely to be a self-deception. If children should react to the arrival of a brother or sister with a more than temporary feeling of loss, the parents have probably overinvested love and attention in them before and have now withdrawn from them love and attention in undue measure.

Sometimes parents are so insecure that they feel threatened by the emergence of a new and separate generation within the family group and for that reason try to weaken the cohesiveness among the siblings. "Divide and conquer" is a principle of warfare to which parents, out of their own neediness, are sometimes driven to their own detriment as well as to the detriment of their children.

The abuse of children as allies in marital conflict can similarly lead to parental interference with a good sibling relationship. Father-daughter alignment versus mother-son alignment is only the most stereotypical form of such interferences. Adults frequently feel that one of their parents have had a good relationship with only one of their siblings and that this left them somehow impoverished and emotionally deprived of a good relationship with that particular sibling in their mature years.

Thus it would seem that the concern of parents over the relationships between their children is negatively biased on cultural as well as on personal grounds. Parents may feel they have created another bridge to immortality, increased their own scope of parental experiences, completed a desirable family unit by adding to it a girl or a boy, but they may also feel they have done all this by diminishing the scope and resources of experiences available to their first child. In the following discussion of the growth-promoting aspects of sibling relationships, we will attempt to show how unrealistic such concerns are and how much mental ease parents could gain by paying more attention to the contribution that siblings make to one another.

In approaching this task, it might be useful if we again suggested that the family is a group of human beings who are essentially unequal. Children are irrevocably separated from their parents by the mere fact of difference in age and, for the only child, also by sex in relation to one parent. To the only child, therefore, the parents inevitably represent very distant, if not unreachable, models. The age difference is too great to allow the child to have much optimism over growing up to achieve the parental stature within the visible or at least manageable future. Optimism about the possibility of growth, however, is one of the most potent and most sustaining attitudes toward life which a child can develop. In this respect an older brother or sister is of tremendous help to a child. Such siblings represent reachable models which are comforting in their imperfections as well as in their achievements. To the eight-year-old, what a brother or sister, age ten, can do is neither unattainable nor overwhelming. It sets a pattern, it gives hope, and most of all, it does not crush. Actually, it may present a challenge to do better, and because of the relatively small age difference and the push provided by physiological maturation, this optimism is likely to prove justified. To reach the particular performance level of a person better endowed than oneself is a difficult assignment for an adult; often it may prove impossible. Between children, differences of endowment can be temporarily blurred by the push of maturation and thus create a hopeful attitude toward life which is likely to be development enhancing no matter what one's congenital gifts and limitations are. Thus, maturation becomes an ally to competition and development.

Parents may often be led to interpret competitiveness between siblings as an expression of unacceptable hostility or at least as a lack of brotherly or sisterly love. Actually, such competitiveness can and probably should frequently be viewed as a growth-stimulating and growth-sustaining interplay of forces. Achievement of an older child may stimulate in the younger the desire to catch up. The achievement of the younger may stimulate in the older the desire to keep up his or her lead. In essence, every sibling plays for the other the role of model as well as the role of the deviant. In healthy development, nobody wants to become exactly like anybody else. One wants to become like the person whom one has used as a model but with certain alterations. In one or another aspect one wants to be better. In other words, siblings are likely to use one another not only as persons to catch up with but also as persons from whom to be different. Competitiveness also takes account of different aptitudes. Competitiveness will lead children to seek out their own potentials of best performance and to cultivate those. In consequence, competitiveness between siblings is not competitiveness for survival—which is destructive to others—but competitiveness directed toward self-fulfillment.

From another perspective, younger brothers and sisters provide the older sibling with his only chances within the family for the experience of a measure of superiority. In relation to their parents, children must always cope with feelings of physiological and intellectual inferiority. The younger brother or sister, on the other hand, sets the older child up as a superior individual within his own generation. Whatever loss of parental attention the younger sibling seems to have caused, his or her late arrival and its consequence undoubtedly offer to many older children a measure of compensation. It is an experience which cannot be provided for the only child no matter how much nursery school, kindergarten, and school experience may offer in terms of opportunities for awareness of one's own potential of being better than others. This superiority of the older child, which rests on the presence of a younger child in the family, offers opportunities of favorable comparison with others, and a younger brother or sister also provides a child with the opportunity to pass on to another the benefit of experiences gained.

In the realm of emotions, the presence of siblings permits the direction of feelings upon more manageable recipients. As mentioned previously, the reaching out of a child toward the parent of the opposite sex can be transferred to a sibling of the opposite sex, but is likely to be diluted in the process and to be stripped of its threatening features. The transference of feelings that are rejected and repulsed by adults to those in the young generation may provide a relationship which is tolerable and transitional. At the same time, this will point the way from the family circle to nonblood-related people to whom sexual reaching out must finally attach itself if development is to follow a healthy direction.

Perhaps even greater is the service which siblings render one another by being available objects of temporary hostility. Hostility expressed toward a sibling is not only less dangerous in the feelings of a child than expression of hostility toward an adult, but it is also limited by parental supervision and is thus secure from the panic that is likely to follow unbridled acting out. Most important, continued family interaction shows that the expression of hostility can be survived without undue damage by the object of the hostility as well as by the one who has expressed it. Fantasies of guilt and punishment cannot run wild, and children who, in their squabbles, hurt one another and make up again, probably become emotionally healthier adults than those who, in their feelings of hostility, have not had similar experiences. Learning that wars lead to peace, that conflicts frequently find a solution, and ultimately that solutions found are no security against the appearance of new conflicts, which in turn must be faced and handled, is a lesson that hardly any human situation can teach more inexpensively and more successfully than the sibling relationship in a nonpathological family.

It is our belief that the wish of parents to have children of both sexes is essentially sound and beneficial to their children. To the little girl, the existence of a brother provides her with an experience of masculinity freed from the connotations of a father figure. Similarly, to the boy in the family, the existence of a sister presents an experience of feminity within the home which does not bear the overpowering impact of adulthood and maternity. Thus brothers and sisters liberate one another to a considerable degree from the anxiety concerning the enigma of the other sex when it is encountered in the formative years only in the person of a parent.

The senior author has frequently observed that siblings, when they speak of one another, use phrases that designate their sex and age position in the family, such as "my older brother," "my younger sister," or vice versa. This has been confirmed by the reports of professional people. It would seem that brothers and sisters furnish one another with reference points for the perception of their own identity. To be different from somebody else not only in terms of such overall categories as parent and child, man and woman, teacher or student, but in terms of people in one's own peer group such as someone among one's classmates, a doctor among doctors, is one of the most important aids in gaining the feeling of identity and self-respect.

Being able to use brothers and sisters as a reference group is of tremendous importance. It provides one of the primary anchors for identity formation in human experience, and it is our suspicion that in our modern search for identity this is a human resource which is not sufficiently tapped because parents discourage it. Here, apparently, concern with equal allocation may interfere greatly with healthy child development because one of the greatest powers which one can derive from identity is the ability to see other people get either more or less than one gets oneself without feeling that one's personality is impaired by this inequality. To know that one is somebody specific, unique, unlike anybody else, not simply the member of a group but a distinctive individual, confers something inviolable upon a human being which fortifies against the adversities of affluence as well as against the adversities of poverty. It is a well-known fact that to have too much, to have a strain of good luck, to be "happy alone," makes people anxious. It is a similarly well-known fact that to have less than others, to be pursued by a series of misfortunes, to fail where others achieve, is experienced as injustice, as threat, as pain. There is practically no way to safeguard human life against such experiences, but to have an identity means to remain essentially unaffected by these encounters with misfortune, and there is hardly any situation in human experience which can help so much in acquiring a sense of identity than the family interaction between siblings.

Not only do these interactions provide the easiest and relatively most enduring experiences of identity, but they also teach children to live with scarcity. Few indeed are the families in which all siblings can be provided materially with all the comforts which their parents would like to see them have. There is no family in which the parents can provide the siblings with all the attention and all the emotional monopolies which the children may want to have. The family is, therefore, a social learning situation par excellence in which children can perceive that one may have to receive less than is potentially available because of the existence of others. It is one of the best situations and strategically one of the first where one can learn that the experience of such differentials means that allocation must be used in terms of equity rather than in terms of equality, and that at least in the long run nobody is hurt by such arrangements and can live on with self-respect and with love of others. In a world in which the task of living is performed more and more in large-scale organizations, in bureaucracies, and in factories, where the positions in the higher status groups become fewer and fewer as the top of the pyramid is approached, learning to live with scarcity without a feeling of self-impairment is one of the most important experiences that can be provided for a growing individual.

If there is any merit in our positive assessment of friction between siblings, it seems to us that some reorientation is needed in parental attitude and reaction to sibling interaction. It suggests that parents might look upon fighting between siblings as growing pains and learning experiences rather than as signs of a relationship disturbance. It might be well for parents to try to discern what follows the quarrels between siblings rather than to focus on the quarrels alone. The positive or negative evaluation of these expressions of conflict rests in essence not on their manifestations but on their resolution. Do these quarrels produce stimuli for growth and identity formation in the children, do they teach the value of settling conflict by compromise, do they seem to lead to permanent estrangement, or are they followed by periods of mutual friendliness and helpfulness?

If children show competitiveness, parents might look to see whether the friction extends to many areas of living or to only a few. If children strive to be better than their brothers and sisters in all areas of experience, the parents might be concerned. If children want to carve out only their own reserve of adequacy or excellence, the parents might want to encourage them.

Parents might also want to consider the relationship of siblings to one another with a view to the future. The fact of organic life makes it likely that most human beings will spend a great portion of their lives after their parents' death. Whatever resource in a child's life a parent may have been, this resource is likely to be lost before the child reaches the end of his or her own life. To have brothers and sisters creates a reserve of human resources derived from one's own childhood family on one's own generational level. To have such additional resources is always helpful. Siblings can also share the burden or the joy of perpetuating the family tree. This responsibility, insofar as it is perceived as such, is therefore lightened. It is a frequent observation that fighting between siblings ceases as they attain adulthood, while mutual support continues to be more or less maintained. This may well be the ultimate reward for one of the perhaps most burdensome requirements of parenthood—patience.

SUGGESTED READINGS

M. Grotjahn, *Psychoanalysis and the Family Neurosis.* New York, W. W. Norton, 1960.

Oscar Lewis, *Five Families.* New York, Basic Books, 1959; *La Vida*, New York, Random House, 1965; *The Children of Sanchez.* New York, Random House, 1961.

Salvador Minuchin et al. *Families of the Slums.* New York, Basic Books, 1967.

Oscar W. Ritchie and Marvin R. Koller, *Sociology of Childhood.* New York, Appleton-Century-Crofts, 1964.

Brian Sutton-Smith and B. G. Rosenberg, *The Sibling.* New York, Holt, Rinehart and Winston, 1970.

Walter Toman, *Family Constellation.* New York, Springer Publishing, 1961.

Frances Ullman, *Getting Along with Brothers and Sisters.* Chicago, Science Research Associates, 1950.

CHAPTER 6

The Half-Concealed Model: Children Observe the Marriage of Their Parents

Children in our culture have very limited opportunities to really observe the marriage of their parents. Marital happiness as well as marital unhappiness frequently conveys itself to them without benefit of adequate explanation or without any explanation at all. However meager their observations, they are the only sources of information with which many children enter their own marriages when they reach maturity. Marriage is, therefore, a half-concealed model. Courses on marriage and the family relationship must of necessity be instructive rather than experiential and their content is frequently as far removed from the reality as a diagram of sexual organs is from the hetersexual experience. Needless to say, many young people enter marriage without even the questionable benefit of instruction received in school.

We are therefore facing the problem that most people marry without adequate experiential or observational information because children are only partly admitted into the marital experience of their parents. They are admitted into the kitchen or the dining room, into the living room and around the house but not into the bedroom when the parents want privacy and, in many instances, not into the bathroom when it is occupied by their parents. They are excluded from physical contact with their parents when they respond to it with signs of sensual stimulation. They are sent to their rooms when their parents want to be together by themselves and, most of all, they are excluded from knowledge about the sexual life of their parents.

Up until recently it was usually the mother who was a routine presence for the children while the father was seen only when he came home from work and during weekend activities. In increasing numbers mothers, too, will often be absent. Children will experience the routine presence of child-care worker and both parents as evening and weekend parents.

By their very presence children limit the freedom of emotional expression between the parents. They may even limit the topics which parents feel free to discuss in the presence of their children. The primal scene is a jealously guarded part of marital privacy, and even if it were witnessed, it would probably be unintelligible to the child. All that the child might perceive are two parents locked in what looks like a physical struggle, an impression frequently strengthened by the sounds which the parents make in ecstasy but which resemble groans of pain. What the child will see in more traditional forms of intercourse is only the back of one parent heaving; his vantage point prevents him from witnessing the ecstasy on the faces of his parents and the actual fusion of their bodies in the genital act. Since many children have sadomasochistic fantasies, the encounter with the primal scene is likely to strengthen such factors in their definition of love in later life. Even when they stumble onto an act of profound intimacy, children may think that they are observing violence and punishment rather than love and orgiastic union. To misunderstand affection for punishment and punishment for affection may be one of the consequences of this unavoidable limitation of the child's observation and effort at understanding.

In many families children also are excluded when the parents discuss trouble. This exclusion is created in part by the separation of work from home. It is difficult to conceal from a farmer's child that economic disaster threatens when the rains do not come or do not stop. Drought and flood cannot be kept from such a child. Financial troubles, however, such as uncollectable rents and debts which one cannot pay, are abstract and can be avoided in conversation in front of children in the hope that the problems may be solved before the children become aware of them. It is part of our culture that, wherever possible, parents try to protect the children against awareness of such difficulties. It is an unrealistic wish of many people that children should be spared awareness of and concern with parental worries. However, children are sensitive to the nonverbal expressions of moods. They can sense problems and they can even sense concealment, reacting to it in exactly the way the parents want to prevent. Exclusion in and by itself may cause anxiety or resentment or both because, ultimately, the message of such parental communication is that the child is too weak to help carry the burdens of the family.

Children may be excluded from the verbal exchanges of their parents by their limited degree of development, but they are usually sensitive enough to body and facial language so that the messages come across, unstated but basically accurate. Children can pick up anxious looks and hostile body positions of the parents without any words being spoken or understood.

They also sense degrees of affection in symbolic expressions. They can feel the difference in love between parents and the love they receive from them. They will sense and compare the two and may find that they do not get enough. The opposite may also be the case: they may sense that the parents do not get enough love from one another and instead seek such love from them. This is the bipolarity of the oedipal experience. Either the child is rejected in his reaching out for a better love or he is encouraged and exploited because of an unsatisfactory love relationship between his parents.

An unfortunate discovery that many children make is that the half-concealed model of their parents' marriage includes half-concealed conflict or struggle. The concealment may have been due to the fact that parents tried to shield their children from their increasingly frequent disagreements and increasingly intense antagonism. If this marital disorganization is at least followed by attempts at union, there is a revival of the hope that the irritation will diminish. The marriage survives and the children observe durability and constancy in the overcoming of estrangement and turmoil.

When, however, the process of estrangement is continued, the negative feelings are not succeeded by positive ones and the marriage is heading for divorce, children are apt to make a potentially most disturbing observation. Close to divorce and after divorce many parents yield to the temptation of talking to their children about their marital unhappiness without restraint while they may have guarded their privacy as long as it was partially rewarding or at least not unmitigated misery. The children of divorce are therefore at risk of becoming more pessimistic about marriage than general experience warrants. A good deal of attention should be given to this experience because the increasing divorce rate will soon make this a developmental challenge to so many children that it will no longer be considered unusual.

It is part of the essence of the half-concealed model that children experience the marriage of their parents solely as it affects them: they experience the marriage as the relationship between two parents rather than as the relationship between two spouses. It comes therefore as a shock or as something not quite intelligible that one of them should not stay on as a parent because he or she does not want to be married anymore. Due to their egotistical orientation, most children will tend to side with the parent who retains custody because the other parent's leaving is experienced as abandonment. The child's natural reaction will be, "How can one of my parents want to leave me?" Perhaps the child's most profound realization is that the divorced parent will no longer be of use to him in times of need.

From the point of view of the child the divorce of parents presents a strange phenomenon of ambiguity and complexity. The parents who leave the home to not really stop being parents by ascription but they stop being parents by function, or at least the way they used to function. Therefore the situation requires a reorientation to them in their new role as host parents on visits rather than as home parents who shared everyday life. They also represent various possibilities of change: they may return, they may acquire custody, or they may marry a stranger with whom the child will have to establish a relationship.

On the other hand, the parents who have custody of the child remain parents as in the past but are now parents of greater complexity because they may bring a stranger into the household to fill a quasi-parental position. If no remarriage occurs, part of the role of the parents who have left the home may be taken on by the remaining parents, who then become overworked with diffused identity and diffused role assumption.

A new experience of children of divorce will be the dating behavior of their single parents who now show signs of social regression. They make dates, they prepare for them, they come home delighted or disappointed, they try to show only the desirable sides of their personality to their new companions—in short, they return to adolescent behavior patterns which seem somewhat inappropriate at this later stage in life. Since most people who have undergone divorce tend to question their attractiveness, a series of unsatisfactory dating experiences may result in a further deterioration of their self-images.

Since in current practice it is usually the mother who retains custody of the children, the new person who enters the family is usually male. This produces certain elements of confusion and also certain risks in the child's developmental experience. The first confusing question which children may ask themselves concerns the reason why mother is nicer to this man than she was to their father and why this relative stranger is nicer to mother than their father was. Children may also experience competition for their affection between their biological father and their mother's new husband. It is natural for the divorced father to want to retain the affection of his children and, similarly, it is natural for a man who marries into a family with children to want to win the affection of these children. In this competition for affection, children may be deprived of effective parenting. They are "dated" by their father and "courted" by their stepfather. Neither dating nor courtship spells discipline or control of oedipal reaching out. The second husband of a divorced mother is not under the constraint of the incest taboo in responding to the budding feminity of a preadolescent or adolescent daughter of his wife. For the son who has to encounter a new man in the house, the Hamlet situation is revived. The oedipal love for the mother that is repressed or defended against by identification with the father thus has a new and much less threatening competitor. To hate him and to wish him dead is not forbidden. As a matter of fact, it may take the rationalization of avenging the father whom he has replaced.

If, in the future, the courts should more frequently give custody of children to fathers, interesting reversals may occur. Male children may either fall in love with their father's second wife or they may feel that they have to avenge their mother who has been replaced by this new woman. Girls may fall in love with their stepfathers and defy the transfer to this situation of constraints which were put on their reaching out for emotional responsiveness from their biological father.

To sum up, when a new spouse—usually male—comes into the household, the children encounter a new object of oedipal wishes in a person who is not protected by the incest taboo and who himself is weakened in his own residual oedipal wishes by his need to show open affection to win the love of his new spouse's children. When this happens to pubescent children they may regress to oedipal desires, and when it happens to older children they may fight constraints with serious developmental risks.

We have focused on the children's experience of divorce largely because its implications are likely to illuminate everything that is solid in a successful marriage. We have two classes of children in our society: children of stable marriages and children of divorce. The child of divorce has more substantial, although biased, information about negative experiences in marriage; the child of a stable marriage has greater ignorance and feelings of exclusion. The choice between negatively biased information and unbiased ignorance is difficult to make. It may be advantageous for a child's development not to know too much, but it is certainly far from ideal to keep the child in such ignorance that he or she will start marriage with unreal expectations. It would seem desirable to give children greater access to the experience of the parents in all types of marriages. An invaluable lesson to be learned is that stability in marriage is to be paid for by repetitive discomforts and that release from a bad marriage is to be paid for by damage to the self-image of the divorced parent and developmental difficulty for the children.

It is frequently said that it is worse for children to grow up in a bad marriage than to grow up in the home of a divorced parent. This statement implies that the bad marriage will be followed by a good marriage or that a single parent is better than two parents in conflict with one another. These assumptions are often neglecting the possibility of turning a bad marriage into a good marriage by changing and nurturing the relationship. They also overlook the risk that a person who has had a bad marriage is likely to select a second marriage partner who resembles the first one in personality and in incompatibility. It need hardly be said that parents owe their children a good marriage, but this is possible only if they can overcome the thinking and feeling of an egotistical child which they have carried into adulthood.

In their own marriages the children of divorce will probably start out with the wish to have a better marriage than their parents did. Some learn from experience, some from observation. Frequently, however, unconscious identification forces the children into a continuation of parental behavior. Actually, what could be called an uncanny law of increment forces many such children as marriage partners into a further deterioration of the negative behavior patterns they have absorbed from their parents. These are situations where the seeking of therapeutic intervention becomes a marital obligation.

This situation, however, is likely to change, particularly for middle class children. It is one of the characteristics of current social change that people of this social group are becoming less and less protective of their privacy. Correspondingly, less and less will be concealed from children and more and more will be observed by children with regard to the marriage of their parents. They may see working mothers as more than just mothers, and fathers as more than just providers. Marriages then will appear to be what they are: not living arrangements between providers and homemakers but privileged continuities of interaction between two persons in a wider context than if they were not so united. Children will witness anger about ascribed sex roles freely expressed where it was formerly concealed, and they will find competence and incompetence in unexpected areas of the marital behavior of their parents. As the half-concealed model becomes less concealed, the results will be dependent on what is done with the increased amount of information. It may contribute to the armamentarium of hostility in marriage, but it may also present a challenge to develop healthier family relationships.

SUGGESTED READINGS

J. L. Despert, *Children of Divorce*. Garden City, N.Y., Doubleday & Co., 1963.

L. Duberman, *The Reconstituted Family: A Study of Remarried Couples and Their Children*. Chicago, Nelson-Hall, 1975.

Judith S. Kestenberg, *Children and Parents*. New York, Jason Aronson, 1975.

Theodore Lidz, *Hamlet's Enemy: Madness and Myth in Hamlet*. New York, Basic Books, 1975.

Herman Nunberg, *Curiosity*. New York, International Universities Press, 1961.

B. Steinzor, *When Parents Divorce*. New York, Pantheon Books, 1969.

CHAPTER 7

Benevolence and Malice in Child Rearing: Children Observe Parental Role Performance

With the convergence of democratic values, progressive education, and psychoanalytic explanations of child development, middle-class parents assume that permissiveness in child rearing is a prerequisite of healthy development. Physiological survival, however, requires limiting care. Parents are therefore faced with a double-bind with regard to child rearing: they are frequently more permissive than they should be, yet they feel that they are not permissive enough. No matter how much parents may be inclined toward permissiveness, the necessity of limiting the activities of their children in order to protect them influence their behavior in the parent-child relationship. The setting of limits, however, is not done anymore with a feeling that it is right and appropriate; it is done apprehensively in fear of stunting a child's growth and development. Nevertheless, however resentful children may be of limitations, they sense that they must have some orientation to boundaries of age-appropriate behavior if they are not to fall subject to a feeling of being neglected or to be faced with challenges that cannot be met.

Child rearing and growing up are bipolar experiences. Being exposed to limiting care is disagreeable but it is also reassuring. Setting limits is uncertain and uncomfortable, but it is also necessary for protective and development-enhancing purposes.

Normally, both discomforts decrease over time and remain active only in pathological parent-child relationships.

Actually, before the first constraining encounter with limiting care, the child has already experienced limitations on his behavior because of physiological immaturity. Not being able to turn one's body when remaining in the same position produces discomfort, and not being able to sit up is one of the first experiences of limits on behavior. When parental care is given, children experience relief from the limitations of their own physical development. This care at the beginning is relieving and not limiting. Only as the body becomes autonomous is parental care experienced as limiting rather than relieving. There is a difficult transition from the earliest period of experiences—being moved because of inability to move oneself, of being burped because of inability to release painful gas, of being fed because of inability to feed oneself—to the post-infantile period when one is forbidden to go where one wants to go, forbidden to defecate wherever and whenever one wants to, and told that it is not nice to belch in the presence of others. In other words, the effect of maturation is the encounter with limiting care. This care must counteract the ignorance of risk and danger in adventures which accompany the child's sense of maturation, which, as in later phases of the life cycle, precedes experience.

Perhaps the outstanding limitation is experienced in that phase of child development in which the child has attained self-directed mobility. Space becomes accessible and at the same time is circumscribed by adult care. The crib, the playpen, and the walking harness are perfect examples of limitations which parents or child-care people impose on maturation. The child must exchange the prison of his or her own former disabilities for a prison of protection. Unfortunately, the protective nature of this prison is not obvious to the child. It is the misfortune of parents that one cannot protect without confinement and that one cannot restrict movement without frustrating a child. Frustration leads to anger and rage; benevolent care is rewarded by angry protests, by tears and tantrums and by attempts to escape the necessary limitations. This protest against benevolence leaves an element of residual malice in everybody which in itself must be coped with as a part of one's development. The criticism of behavior implicit in parental discipline and later, parental disagreement with their children's claims of autonomy keeps alive this element of anger against limiting care and this probably explains human resistance to authority throughout the whole life cycle in many instances.

Frequently, not only is limiting care experienced as discomfort, but when it is inconsistently or even capriciously imposed, it can be confusing as well. Furthermore, when parents and schools resort to punishment for violation of the limits which they have had to set, they must frequently reverse formerly used procedures for expressing care. Children who in the past were comforted by parental presence are sent up to their rooms; in school they are made to stand in a corner. Discipline that is meant to be protection is experienced as punishment and in its symbolic meaning as a reversal of care. Thus limiting care is experienced as non-care. The child's lack of understanding of the benevolent nature of limiting care in any of its forms leads to a pervasive experience of interference with growth. This situation is sometimes aggravated by the observation that older siblings may do what one may not do or that younger siblings enjoy more permissiveness than one enjoyed when one was the only child.

Resentment and malice with which children react to limiting care, however, are not the only major emotional aspects of the relationship between parents and children. Most children are aware that their parents love them and that they are sources of joy and concern to their parents. Similarly, most parents know that the children are too immature to understand the protective meaning of limiting care and, therefore, can cope with the expressions of anger and frustrations with which these limits are met. In many families the basic love and the sense of not being understood exist side by side for both children and parents for the rest of their lives. Needless to say, it would be desirable if the lack of rapport could come to an end when sons and daughters reach young adulthood and would not be renewed in reverse when older sons and daughters become caretakers of their aged parents.

One might summarize the above by identifying three stages of the experience of care. At first, care relieves the limitations of an incompletely developed and therefore dysfunctional organism. As the body matures, care reaches a new phase in which it becomes limiting to a functional human being in order to protect him against physically dangerous risk taking. In the third stage, care is exercised in relation to the social behavior and the mental life of sons and daughters.

Once the element of anger and malice unavoidably connected with the experience of growing up is established, it is likely to go into the unconscious of most children because anger directed against parents when first experienced is too dangerous to remain conscious. In adolescence it may return to consciousness because with parents who are no longer physically or mentally superior, one can afford to be consciously angry. Since one does not need protection and limiting care anymore, such attempts at care by parents become obsolete and are thought to justify rebelling, which is supported by society and frequently diverted into other outlets, such as political radicalism, refutation of a parent's supervision by choosing a profession or occupation considered unsuitable by the parents, or marrying someone of whom the parents disapprove.

Since adolescents find it harder and harder to rebel against adult, and particularly parental, authority without finding some support in public or private education, the only possible rebellion for some is change of consciousness because almost anything else is considered variance rather than deviance. Thus whil permissive parents feel that they are not being permissive enough, their sons and daughters are rebelling and feel that they are not rebelling enough.

In adulthood resentment and malice generated by the parents during childhood may also return from the unconscious and may become directed against their own offspring. This may be stimulated and justified by the difficult demands of providing limiting care. In some cases the existence of hostility may be denied by being oversolicitous. On the other hand, it may find expression in the physical violence leading to instances of battered children which currently receive so much national attention.

In some ways children in population groups in which protest or violation of limiting care is punished by physical discipline are liberated sooner from these limitations than children in population groups where discipline is essentialy verbal. A mother whose daughter is taller than she and a father whose son has become stronger than he is very likely to stop limiting care because they will not risk danger and humiliation in its exercise. Once the bodies of children become physically equal or superior to the bodies of their parents, limiting care of the purely physical kind comes to an end.

Verbal expression of limiting care knows no such boundaries: this is the price which many middle-class children have to pay for not having been physically punished by their parents. Middle-class parents do not know when to stop exercising verbal limiting care because they do not perceive any risk in being defeated with the same degree of clarity as in administering the physical kind. Verbal discipline is likely to produce guilt, and guilt can be kept alive in an adult son or daughter by a parent who, though failing physically, retains this psychological power. In other words, middle-class people are more likely not to know when to stop parenting.

Such continuous parenting is particularly irritating because it frequently turns the original misunderstanding of limiting care as a stupid exercise of power into a correct evaluation. In times of rapid social change, parental ways of coping with the challenges of life frequently become obsolete. Changes in acceptable standards of behavior bypass parental perception, and when parents of sons and daughters who have attained adulthood express criticism and concerns which show their ignorance of such changes, they become counterproductive as well as irritating.

This chapter, however, should not close on this negative note. Even irritating and confusing care expresses attention and concern. It pleases the egotism of the child, or the child in the adult. It satisfies frequently residual dependency needs, it assures sons and daughters that they are significant and relevant to their parents at every age. The anger created by frustration, which all limitation implies, is therefore likely to become submerged in the unconscious, or failing that, results in ambivalence rather than rejection of the parents. Such ambivalence, however, is very likely to be an aid in becoming a well-functioning adult.

SUGGESTED READINGS

Jules Henry, *Pathways to Madness*. New York, Vintage Books, 1973.
Theodore Lidz, *The Person*. New York, Basic Books, Revised edition 1976.

Theodore Lidz, Alice Cornielson, Dorothy Terry and Stephen Fleck, "The Transmission of Irrationality" in T. Lidz et al. *Schizophrenia and the Family.* New York, International Universities Press, 1963.

Margaret Mead, *Male and Female.* New York, W. W. Norton, 1939.

Parenthood, it Psychology and Psychopathology. E. James Anthony, M. D. and Therese Benedek, M. D., eds., Boston, Little, Brown and Company, 1970.

Jean Piaget, *Judgment and Reasoning in the Child.* translated by C. Gattengo and F. M. Hodgson, New York, W. W. Norton, 1962.

Robert R. Sears, Eleanor Maccobi and Harry Levin, *Patterns of Child Rearing.* Evanston, Ill., Row, Peterson & Co., 1957.

PART III

The Restless Changes
of Adulthood

CHAPTER 8

Leaving Childhood: Adolescence and Youth

It is commonplace that adolescents have a difficult time them-selves and give difficult times to their parents, teachers, and friends. At this stage in life they are faced with conflicts about dependency and separation. Physical maturation as well as social expectations demand or at least suggest separation as a developmental goal, but psychologically adolescents are frequently not ready to face the loneliness of, for instance, the strange world of a college campus a distance from their home. Every Dean of Students knows the freshmen who cannot bring themselves to attend classes, who stay in the dormitories and are afraid to meet the new world in which they are supposed to behave with competence and equanimity. In the beginning there are frequent telephone calls home and feelings of incompetence in self-maintenance and protection of one's time from invasion by others, as well as feelings of inadequacy in establishing relationships.

These feelings of apprehension which one frequently encounters in adolescents are by no means unjustified. At that time and also in early adulthood, young people must prepare themselves to make important decisions about both loving and making a living. Relationship decisions and occupational and professional deci-sions preoccupy their minds and sometimes interfere with the social role of being an adequate college student, who is attentive in class and can concentrate on studies, as well as having a good time when others do. The first of these two major decisions which have to be made constitutes one of the central themes of family life: the preparations for loving one person who is to become one's spouse and the parent of one's children. In our society, where the selection of a marriage partner is based on romantic love and not on negotiations by more experienced people such as parents and marriage brokers, learning to love one person is one of the most important tasks of this stage of development. In the emotional relationship experience, therefore, the adolescent has to perform two functions: the separation from his parents and the preparation for union with an adult.

The process is gradual and frequently characterized by the experience of at least temporary failure because the love of children for their parents is primarily egotistical and does not provide an adequate basis for loving in the sense of giving, caring and strengthening or, perhaps most of all, assigning priority to the well-being of the other over the well-being of oneself.

This period of learning to love actually starts in pubescence, between the ages of eleven and twelve, a period in which the body matures ahead of psychological and social capacities. Girls may experience their early menstrual periods not as a gratifying onset of womanhood but as something frightening. The earlier experience of losing blood as the result of a cut finger or a bruised kneecap has prepared the child to connect bleeding with injury and it is difficult to reorient onself to monthly bleeding as an experience of healthy maturation. The early connection of bleeding with injury is made also by males and fills them with awe and apprehension about this aspect of womanhood with which they will have to learn to live. It is one of the many aspects of the enigma that women present to men and, in many cases, also to themselves. Boys may be confused or terrified by their first wet dreams, not only because of the newness of the experience but because, here again, early experiences have established connections between yellow secretions and pus. Since education can never substitute for experience, there is really no way of preparing girls and boys for these experiences which they must work through for themselves, aided more or less by the sometimes incorrect explanations of age and sex mates. Freeing sexual maturation from the symbolism of disease or disorder is therefore one of the major problems of development.

In our society, where marriage is frequently separated by a decade or more from the onset of physiological readiness, the process is probably unduly prolonged and complicated by premature stimulation. Girls develop crushes on entertainers, developing fantasies of love for males who are by definition inaccessible because they are commercially packaged rather than real. Boys and girls discover pornography, which connects the idea of loving and sex with the idea of ugliness. This is probably one of the most unfortunate approaches of our so-called liberated and revolutionary youngsters to sexual experience. Since the sexual organs are not in and of themselves aesthetic, the frequent displays of a female figure with spread legs and hands pointing to the vagina are hardly likely to link the heterosexual experience with beauty. The displays of the male body with exposed penis cannot help doing the same for girls, and one is tempted to think that the consumers of pornography are unconsciously punishing themselves for repressed sexual wishes: having been rejected in the reaching out for the parent of the other sex, they now find visual ugliness where there were formerly prohibitions and infantile perversions. It was one of Freud's great discoveries that children in early childhood develop sensual satisfactions and relationship preferences which in an adult would be designated as perversion such as love of one's feces and sadomasochistic gratification. These wishes and fears of punishment for having them frequently go into the unconscious before oedipal fantasies find their hiding place there.

Confused by new romanticism and old terror, adolescents have to start on the long road to developing the capacity for mature love. The delay between the beginning and the completion of this process has advantages and disadvantages. It permits throught testing before one is confronted with the actual experience. From thought testing, adolescents must, and do, proceed to partial body testing and, finally, intercourse, which usually precedes the experience of mature love. This stage of singlehood is a gradual and often uncomfortable process of finding out about the physical implications of love and relationships. Where the body pushes and society delays, mental life is often negatively affected. Sex without love and without any intent of commitment is doomed to fail because a permanent commitment is the ultimate expression of release from the destiny of separation and incompleteness; if one wants to preserve separation and feels one's own incompleteness as a protection from commitment, sex will inevitably be disappointing. Sex without love is essentially only a manipulation of the other for one's own purposes.

Parents cannot offer guidance in these experiences because they point to the impending separation of their children from the home. They are usually beyond middle age or close to middle age when their sons and daughters are adolescents, so that many of them unconsciously resent the flowering of a new life, however awkward and conflicted, because it reminds them of the fact that they are past or about to pass their prime and that the road for them is downhill. There is a drama in the fact that uphill development is just as difficult as downhill development and that parents have to experiment with adaptation to the latter while their children must do so with the former. To see a son or daughter experiment or not experiment with learning mature love is equally disquieting for parents. If the child fails to grow up to be an adult person, it is likely to be considered their failure. If he or she succeeds, they will lose many of the gratifications of a parent-child relationship. In other words, while adolescents are struggling to learn to exercise their power, the parents, though powerless, feel they must help them; they have not accepted as yet that separation means loss of their own power and that they can retain this power only at the price of family conflict and of making the development of the child more difficult than it need be. Another diffiuclty in this situation is created by the fact that most adolescents are still dependent financially on their parents and must seek their help in some decision making and return to them from time to time for familial security. Parents are often accused that they do not let go of their children. The accusation that children do not let go of their parents has equal validity.

From body testing many adolescents move to relationship testing, from dating to going steady, from going steady in high school to sleeping with somebody in college, from sleeping with somebody to living together, and then to marriage. It is in adolescence that narcissistic immaturity most frequently inflicts psychic wounds on others and on self.

Adolescents may have learned to establish relationships of friendship without the need for sexual union. They have frequent relationships with persons of the same sex without the challenge of attaining closeness through union. These are based on distance and similarity rather than on the experience of closeness and living with differences. Being less intense, these relationships are not subjected to the severe tests of heterosexuality and commitment. Being less intense and less tested, they are likely to be more stable than the relationships with a person of the other sex who is potentially a marriage partner and a challenge to one's ability to put the well-being of the other above one's own and, potentially, to commit oneself to do this for a lifetime.

Adolescent love is transitional love. The adolescent starts out with the essential egotism of the child and remains resistant for a considerable amount of time to transcending his egotism and to giving care to other people. The hard lesson to learn in adolescence is the realization that a relationship must be based on reciprocity rather than on exploitation. It must be learned that every date can develop into a relationship if the encounter makes both people feel that they have something to give to the other. In the beginning, adolescents on a date usually think only of what they can get; they are essentially two inexperienced exploiters trying to outwit each other. Even after they have learned to be more concerned with giving than with receiving, they may still be frightened of long-term commitments because they may feel that their power of giving is still too limited and that their egotism is still too strong to exclude the search for opportunities of finding a more giving partner.

It can be frequently observed that early relationships break up because of small disagreements or separation in space or time, or simply because of fantasies about gaining a better experience through another encounter. Finally, dissatisfaction with the heterosexual experience as such, the shock of finding that relationships do not spell continuous happiness, or simply a vague feeling of not being ready may account for the many breakups that produce one heartache after another and the repeated experience of what seems every time to be a permanent loss.

It is not only the breakup itself which, at least for one of the two people involved, produces a feeling of being hurt, damaged, and betrayed, but also the recovery afterwards that is difficult. Young people are often unable to compartmentalize an experience, and a trauma can affect their whole life. An adolescent who cannot return to his books when his love partner is unfaithful or wants to leave him entirely feels totally disabled. Where disorganization is not followed by reorganization, we have pathology, and professional help may be necessary to restore the course of social development.

Attempts at self-repair usually focus on finding a new partner for relationships, but this is an attempt beset with risks. The selection of a partner when one is on the rebound is frequently made not on the basis of affinity or a sense of love but essentially for egotistic reasons and, therefore, is likely to lead to a repetition of the experience. When one engages in a relationship on such a basis, one is likely to select a partner merely because one happens to be available; such a partner may also be on the rebound and therefore, the response will also be egotistical.

Such rebounds will not occur as a result of disappointment over loss of relationship if the adolescent has learned that a relationship failure is not a total failure. Even linguistically the word "rebound" suggests that one wants to be bound again. If one is not mature enough, however, to tolerate earlier bonds, it is unlikely that new ties will be found to be more satisfactory. After relationship failure one needs to change one's relationship behavior if one wants to avoid new and more depressing disappointments. In rebound arrangements one partner objectifies the other; he uses the other essentially as an object to satisfy his own needs for repair, for company, possibly even for social prestige. In such relationships the focus of attention is self and not the other.

The pain of breakup, however, is worthwhile if it ennobles—in other words, if the suffering is turned into a struggle to conquer egotism and to replace it by altruism or at least readiness for reciprocity. In early relationships one does not conceive of the need to change for others. Only if one sees and feels that the other is not object but subject is one ready for mature love.

Unfortunately, the task of the adolescent of changing egotistical love into mature love is hampered by cultural influences. Love

songs suggest either permanent bliss or permanent sadness. Adver-
tisements for cosmetics and even cars suggest that one can win love
and retain love through gimmicks—in other words, with little or
no effort, without doing things for the other. Nothing in our
popular entertainment suggests that early relationships cannot be
love but are, instead, a learning experience and represent more
tests rather than true attachment. In this process of testing, young
people invite deception from each other. On dates one presents a
false front, one puts one's best foot forward, one fakes interest
where none is felt, one deceives even oneself about the expectations
of the other. Going steady is in itself a deception because it implies
that the time spent with only one person, the dating partner, is a
commitment of some duration. Testing by living together is a
measure of correction of the early deceptions involved in dating
and going steady. It exposes the relationship to reality, to routine,
and to the inevitable disappointments and irritations of living with
differences in closeness. There is a tremendous difference between
going out together and waking up together in the morning. There is
irritation in sharing a bathroom. Perhaps most important, there is
irritation even in attempting to deceive oneself and the other about
one's disappointments. One cannot maintain this conscious effort
all the time and will have to show oneself as disappointed and
irritated. For these reasons, romantic love is likely to be only partly
satisfactory as a basis for a lasting relationship because it starts
with the assumption of uninterrupted happiness and, because of its
fairy-tale quality, must lead to disenchantment in the confronta-
tion with reality.

In mature love one can maintain relationships, tolerate disappointments and irritations by thinking of the other before thinking
of oneself. One must have achieved psychological separation from
parents or at least a capacity for resolving ambivalence about
separation from the parents in favor of a relationship with a person
of one's own generation. One must have realized that happiness of
the other is the basis for one's own happiness, one must be able to
put an end to conflict with the partner when it occurs, and one
must be able not to wait for the other to make the first move. In
other words, one's egotism must have become "tired" and one's
capacity for relationship must have come into being. The motiva-
tion for this process of change is unhappiness in singlehood.

There are people, however, who are afraid of greater unhappiness in marriage because they feel themselves too vulnerable to incur its risks. They may also feel that they cannot have their self-realization inhibited by the demands of commitment or the conflicts of dual-career marriages. Such people stay single. For them singlehood is not a transition but a permanent lifestyle. By choosing to remain single, however, they do not remain exempt from the demands made by their aging parents. If they attain a measure of satisfaction out of protecting their vulnerability or self-realization, they may lead very satisfactory lives but they will do so at the price of not having the gratification of meeting the challenge of differences and the challenge of union and separation repetitively over the life cycle.

SUGGESTED READINGS

Adolescence: Psychosocial Perspectives. G. Caplan and S. Lebovici, eds., New York, Basic Books, 1969.

Peter Blos, *On Adolescence: A Psychoanalytic Interpretation.* Glencoe, Ill., Free Press, 1961.

Daedalus. *Twelve to Sixteen: Early Adolescence.* Joseph Adelson et al, Fall 1971.

Erik H. Erikson, *Identity, Youth and Circle.* New York, W. W. Norton, 1968.

Erich Fromm, *The Art of Loving.* New York, Bantam Books, 1963.

Issues in Adolescent Psychology. Dorothy Rogers ed., New York, Appleton-Century-Crofts, Educational Division, Meredith Corporation, 1969.

Irene M. Josselyn, *The Adolescent and His World.* New York, Family Service Association of America, 1952.

Kenneth Keniston, *The Uncommitted: Alienated Youth in American Society.* New York, Harcourt, Brace and World, 1965.

John Barron Mays, *The Young Pretenders.* London, Michael Joseph, 1965.

Normal Adolescence: Its Dynamics and Impact. Formulated by the Committee on Adolescence Group for the Advancement of Psychiatry, New York, Charles Scribner's Sons, 1968.

Daniel Offer, M.D. and Judith Baskin Offer, *From Teenage to Young Manhood.* New York, Basic Books, 1975.

CHAPTER 9

Adulthood: Responsibility for One's Own Development

The statement that life and development can be divided into distinct stages is frequently made for reasons of convenience and clarity of description. In reality, one stage of development leads into another and during its own course passes through various phases. In the preceding chapter we have identified the main theme of adolescence as ambivalence between a return to childhood dependency and movement toward separation from one's parents. This stage also involves an approximation of independence which in turn will have to be partly given up in order to establish a relationship with a person of one's own generation which will form the anchor of one's existence.

In contrast to adolescence, adulthood can be defined as a period of relative freedom from ambivalence about growth. It represents the maximum degree of resistance to regression under stress that we experience during our life cycle. It may last a long time but it will not last forever. Certainly the concept of adulthood, like that of any other period of development, should not suggest freedom from the need to learn ever-new adaptations and freedom from the temptation to regress.

Most of all, adulthood is perhaps the awareness that one has choices rather than limitations. Like coping with limitations, coping with choices also presents difficulties and a test of one's abilities and one's competence. Choice implies not only the possibility of the attainment of the desirable but also the giving up of other desirables that are incompatible with what one has decided to choose. Furthermore, choice implies the risk of failure and, therefore, the possibility of self-reproach, of narcissistic wounding, and the task of self-repair if one has chosen wrongly. Because of this complexity of choice, courage is required and one's decision should reflect this courage to go forward in one's own development rather than to seek comfort and security in going backwards. Adulthood is the ability to risk oneself with courage rather than with trepidation, and also, even more importantly, in spite of trepidation. There is no courage where no danger is apparent. People who do not see danger are more likely fools than heroes.

Because of all this, adulthood is a period of cultivating one's own development. This is perhaps the greatest responsibility but also the greatest opportunity of adulthood. From birth to late adolescence our development has been cultivated by others: parents, institutionalized child care, the school system, peer pressure. All these have been essentially external forces promoting or conceivably impeding our development. This responsibility is transferred in adulthood from others to self. Now the main task of understanding is not other-directed but self-directed. A child, however, young, must understand, at least minimally, the directions of the adults who care for him, constrain him, and surround him with limiting care. An adolescent in the process of separation has to understand the personal and parental forces which hold him back in this process. Once the process is completed, the task of understanding becomes essentially self-understanding because it is now the self that is determining growth or regression. Self can become one's friend or one's enemy. This understanding must encompass childhood residues as well as adult elements in one's behavior. When childhood residues dominate, one's self will not stand up well under the demands made upon adults.

During childhood one has learned to order the world and one's relationship to it in terms of being subjected to limiting care as well as by being inhibited by inadequate capacities of understanding. To be sure, these inadequacies of understanding lessen as one grows older. Still, one enters upon adulthood with a large backlog of experiences of feeling misunderstood and of not quite understanding why one should be so consistently misunderstood. In adulthood the constraints of limiting care disappear, and this freedom puts the burden upon the adult to be responsible for himself and to correct his misunderstandings or at least his feelings of being misunderstood. Where the constraints put up by others have lost their power, one has to build one's own constraints and to order one's own world in order not to fall into the despair of indecision and confusion caused by the lack of boundaries. One cannot replace the norms of others by one's own anomie. In consequence, one has to develop a new ability to test one's attempts at understanding, to reach conclusions from these tests and to make decisions which cannot be based on either the guidance of others or rebellion against them. Instead of learning from the mistakes or through the mistakes of others, one must now learn through one's own mistakes. He who cannot learn from his own mistakes will not be able to cope with the challenges of adulthood and maturity, will probably fail in his relationships with others, and will at one point or another feel either the need for therapeutic assistance or the shadows of depression.

The testing of relationships and professional choices in adulthood is different from the testing in adolescence in the implication of commitment and the amount of time that one will give to see whether the test works out. In adulthood one must test on a long-term basis because if one were to test the results of decisions on a short-term basis, one would be permanently faced with the price of overinvestment. One cannot go to law school for three years or study medicine for four years and longer in order to see in a six-month test whether this is what one wants to do for a lifetime. One does not get married, establish a home, and have children in order to find out after a short period of time that this is not the most desirable lifestyle. The essence of adult testing is therefore responsible testing in terms of giving time a chance. The cause of much suffering for adolescents and their parents is the failure of adolescents to give a chosen test the time to mature and prove, by its longtime results, whether the decision was right or wrong. This observation of the time difference in testing between adolescence and adulthood is probably based on the still egotistical nature of adolescent testing. An adolescent does not consider what the test will cost other people; he is only concerned with the cost to himself. As one attains adulthood, one becomes concerned about the possibility that a test quickly ended may hurt somebody and this will by itself produce more endurance in testing and more patience in awaiting results. Although it is still self-testing, it is altruistic in the sense that the effect of the test on others will determine its duration as well as its evaluation. Where this does not happen, the adult is still acting as an adolescent.

The longtime implications of decision making in adulthood could seduce us into thinking that the capacities to pass these tests successfully should be fully developed before embarking on experiential ventures. It is obviously impossible to determine by tests and even more impossible to determine by self-assessment whether one has attained the competence for professional decision making, meeting the challenges of marriage, and making a decision in favor of parenthood. The test comes in the experience and is likely not to land the tester in the highest bracket of achievement. It will be shown in the chapters that follow where the difficulties and fallacies of such testings lie and to what degree the consequences of failing the first test can be repaired by continued development. We are returning to our initial observation that the phase of adulthood is also a process of growth and, conceivably toward its end, a process of decline. The essence of competence in adult testing lies in the ability to draw on earlier experiences in coping with the new. It is an integrative process and also a time-testing process. While the adolescent is experimenting with jobs and people on a sporadic basis, the adult is experimenting with processes of commitment to jobs and people. In this process he will also never or very rarely have the experience of complete competence but he will always have the feeling of confidence that justifies continued testing. To repeat, while the child and the adolescent are constrained and essentially fearful, the adult is free of constraint and must have an element of courage which is not required of the child or adolescent.

SUGGESTED READINGS

Most books relating to Adulthood deal with Marriage or Parenthood and our suggestions for additional reading will be found at the end of the chapters dealing with these aspects of development. Here we can only suggest:

Barbara Fried, *The Middle Age Crisis.* New York, Haper & Row, 1967.
Group for the Advancement of Psychiatry. *The Educated Woman: Prospects and Problems.* Mental Health Materias Center, New York, 1975.
Gail Sheehy, *Passages: Predictable Crises of Adult Life.* New York, Dutton, 1976.

CHAPTER 10

Marriage:
Lifestyle or Transition?

It is an indestructible myth that one marries for happiness. This myth is maintained by the well-known fairy tale ending, "and they were married and lived happily ever after." No observation of parental marriages, no observation of the marriages of friends, not even the experience of an unhappy marriage which ends in divorce seems to defeat this myth. Since the myth is so resistant to counterevidence, it probably expresses a deep need.

In reality, happiness in marriage requires wisdom and understanding to be maintained. What one really gains from marriage is relief of loneliness. One has the benefit of intimate company in lieu of passing and possibly nonsexual relationships. The closeness is presumed to be durable. If people find that this is possible, their marriage will express the experience that it is better to be together than to be alone in spite of irritation, disappointment, and annoyance in the discovery that one's marriage partner is not what one expected a spouse to be.

Another basis for possible happiness lies in the developmental challenge which every marriage represents. This first involves the overcoming of the conflict between old and new loyalties. One must change loyalties in a marriage if it is to work because spouses start out as relative strangers to one another. People can have any amount of premarital heterosexual felicity and still start as strangers in marriage. They bring roughly two decades or more of separate developmental experience into a situation demanding a measure of harmony and closeness. Loyalty to the new marriage partner requires that one try to change one's strangeness into something with which the other can become familiar. This change somehow involves changing what one's parents approved of into something that will meet the approval of one's spouse. This means that in some way one is asked to commit an identity change and thereby an emotional betrayal. Moreover, one is rewarded for this betrayal by the approval which our society still bestows on marriages which spell permanence.

The difficult separation from the parents which began so tentatively at the end of childhood and the start of adolescence ideally receives its final resolution in marriage. It provides the synchronization of psychological development and social capacities with physiological maturation. People who cannot find their most important association in a commitment to another adult are at the risk of remaining hampered or disabled in the attainment of full adulthood. The married person who continues to think of his parents as anchor points of existence has failed in meeting a major challenge of adulthood.

In a marriage people find protection from the likelihood of greater misery at the price of exposure of one's vulnerability to another person who, as has been suggested, is in most instances a stranger—at least physiologically, but very likely also psychologically and developmentally. The evaluation of a marriage must be based on the relief of loneliness and on the lessening power of residual egotism. This evaluation culminates in the answer to the question, "Is it better for the other to be my spouse than not?" Those who would phrase this question, "Is it better for *me* to be married to that person or not?" probably have not reaped the developmental benefit of a mature marriage, because a marriage in which the priority is still egotistically the self rather than the other is likely to remain immature, fragile and disappointing to the point where divorce seems to be the better alternative.

People who think primarily of what they will get out of a relationship for themselves cannot stay together. The essential reorientation from adolescence to adulthood is to consider what one can give to the other. This, however, is no guarantee of a lasting commitment and a mature happiness, because what one has to give may not be acceptable to the other, for conscious or unconscious reasons. In such cases divorce may also be a better alternative. It is also very important to note in this context that two people usually have different potentials for giving, so that the exchange will not be on an equal basis. One or the other will get more, one or the other will get less. Exchanges in marriage are not those of equality but those of equity. A degree of mutuality must exist if a marriage is to last on an other than pathological basis. Nobody can well continue in a marriage with the feeling of being unrewarded for his or her input.

Relationships require cultivation and are dependent on the changes that the process of maturation and aging brings out in the partners within the relationship. At the beginning of a relationship, particularly that of marriage, the first concern is probably the overcoming of disappointment about the disparity between fantasy and reality. Expectations usually exceed fulfillments. People frequently reveal physiological and psychological impairments which they have either managed to conceal before the intimacy of marriage or have developed in the course of the marriage. A marriage is therefore exposed to new disappointments at every stage of its cycle.

In the case of mature love, the primary concern is the need to help the other to feel better about himself or herself than he or she did before the marriage. It is one of the essentials of cultivating a relationship to send affirmative signals, to be more concerned about the positive aspects of the partner than about his or her negative aspects, and to be more concerned about the other's growth than about one's own. In the later phases of a marriage it is similarly more important to be concerned about the partner's maintenance of an adequate self-image than about one's own. If one concentrates on the other more than upon self, one is likely to receive more in return, and even aging becomes easier.

It is frequently suggested and recommended by marriage counselors that cultivating the marital relationship requires open and, by implication, full communication. This proposition has a very sound basis in theory, but in reality it cannot and probably should not be fully honored. Since at the beginning of the marriage the two spouses find one another relative strangers, they have to make it possible for one another to become acquainted beyond the level made possible by courtship, engagement, and premarital intercourse. At this stage, many marital experiences are of a disappointing character. It is questionable whether a beginning relationship can tolerate full disclosure of the disappointment which one causes the other because even specific objections carry the risk of being received as global rejection. The message, "You are not what I expected," however tactfully put, is likely to receive a negative response or a reciprocal expression of disappointment, creating negative feelings on both sides. Frequently it implies a belated discovery of deception and has an element of accusation. It is naive to assume that when people tell one another of their dissatisfactions with their marriage that afterwards they will find it easy to correct what is disappointing in them. Frequently it is not even possible to reveal to the other the extent or the cause of one's disappointment. It may have unconscious roots and may express itself only in body signals of a vague feeling of discontent or anxiety, and specific and acceptable responses cannot be given.

Most important for communication to strengthen a relationship is the readiness of the two marriage partners to admit the legitimacy of the needs of each other. We return to the old problem of egotism versus altruism. If one is concerned only with one's own needs, one will find little legitimacy in the needs of the other if they are incompatible with one's own. Communication is like a sharp knife. It should be used only by skillful hands and only sparingly. Most of all, it should be used only between people whose love is so strong that it can withstand the infliction of hurt and ego damage. It is unfortunate that it is frequently recommended where such love has disappeared or, at least, is in jeopardy.

Perhaps even more important, the demand for full communication denies the respect for the other's privacy. Wanting to know all about the other and feeling wronged if such knowledge is not volunteered is an expression of invasiveness. It is usually evaluated as unmindful of personal feelings by the other, disregarding one's right to privacy, and a disregard of the territory and boundaries about which each partner should have autonomy in marriage.

Ultimately, communication codifies and thereby gives a quality of permanence to feelings which may be temporary. They may be temporary for the one who communicates, they may be permanent for the recipient of the communication. Even where communication is desirable, time for reception of a communication may not be available when it is wanted. In more traditional arrangements husbands frequently came home still preoccupied with the experiences of a day in the office and found wives preoccupied with their experiences in the home and in relation to childrearing. Each would be bursting to tell the other about his or her day. Consequently, neither would find nor provide a listener. The same situation exists in different forms in modern times. Where husband and wife both work, they come home preoccupied with experiences of the working place. Neither may be able to listen to the other because they are still listening to themselves in order to sort out the experiences of the day. Communication attempts may, in both instances, have a sham quality. People may pretend to listen to one another out of courtesy or even out of love, but they may not be able to pay full attention because previous experiences have not released them for attentiveness to one another. It would be a wise marriage in which the people who want to communicate with one another would first of all make sure whether the other is psychologically and maybe physiologically ready to receive the communication.

The need for privacy and difficulties in communication are heightened by the fact that modern times have produced a separation of the working place from the home, and for two working spouses, separation of their working places. This adds to modern marriages the experience of being alone when one would prefer the company of the other. This is ultimately an experience of separation where union is wanted and, as a result, tests a person's ability to cope with separation even in the marriage situation which suggests union, its possibility, its desirability, and its promise. Every marriage partner will frequently experience discomfort at being alone when he would want his spouse to be present. One spouse may have an occupation which requires his absence in the evenings, another may have an occupation which requires his absence from the home during daytime hours. This presents a risk to the one who is at home and feels lonely because such a vacuum has a tendency to be filled by people other than one's spouse.

It is quite possible that the increase of our divorce rate is due not only to dissatisfaction in marriage but to the fact that people who experience loneliness in marriage meet many potential substitutes for their spouses outside of home, particularly in working places. There is a great difference between meeting a potential substitute for one's spouse on social occasions and meeting a possible substitute routinely every day in social interactions demanded by apparently non-emotional role requirements. Since every marriage has its dissatisfactions, positive fantasies develop toward people whom one encounters on the job and who are not tested in the reality of intimacy and marriage. Such fantasies, thus, present a grave threat to existing marriages. Fantasy is stimulated by uncommitted encounter and may invite commitment.

If both spouses were tempted at the same time to follow the call of a new encounter and if there were no children, it might be quite acceptable for these people to learn from the disappointments of the new encounter that it is time to stop their egotistical fantasies about marriage. They might realize that their first marriage was only a transitory experience and anticipatory socialization which paved the way for better relationship cultivation in their second marriages. It might be a valuable lesson to find out that new constellations are not better than old ones and that something other than the changing of constellations is required for a measure of happiness in marriage, namely, readiness for changing one's own behavior pattern. If no such readiness is attained, we are facing the tragedy of one immature experimentation with marriage following another and so on until depression sets in and people give up the striving for maturity.

Probably the strongest experience of loneliness in marriage lies in the phenomenon of ambivalence. One finds oneself frequently in a situation in which one would prefer to feel nothing but love, but in the reality of human existence, it is very difficult to maintain such total constancy of affection for another. Out of compassion or courtesy, if for no other reason, one usually suppresses the negative side of the ambivalence in the interaction with one's marriage partner. In this respect, each partner is alone with himself and love has produced loneliness.

In summary, modern marriages seem to require that the partners be able to tolerate three types of loneliness. One is the loneliness created by the physical absence of the partner due to modern conditions. The second is the loneliness created by the fight with one's fantasies about finding a better partner. Finally, there is the loneliness created by the solicitude which spares the other any communication of negative feelings. In coping with these three types of loneliness one essentially is faced with the problem of renunciation or of lowering one's aspiration level by giving up one's insistence on satisfaction while leaving the wish intact. Both forms of coping imply change of self rather than change of the other and are thus expressions of mature love and skill in the cultivation of relationships.

One of the greatest developmental challenges in marriage is the task of separating the marriage partner from his symbolic meaning as a parental figure. Many women have maternal attitudes toward their husbands, and at least in former times many husbands, being usually older than their wives, had paternal attitudes toward their wives. Where separation from parents has not been completed, these factually nonincestuous qualities produce unconscious incestuous apprehension and may interfere with a satisfactory heterosexual relationship between the spouses. Even greater difficulties can occur when children are used as functional parent figures by their own fathers and mothers.

In the course of time spouses usually manage to separate one another from parental symbolism. However, it is frequently more difficult for a woman to separate her spouse behavior from the tendency to repeat maternal behavior which she experienced as a child. In restaurants it is frequently possible to observe a woman offering food from her plate to her escort by holding a fork or spoon under the nose of her male partner as if she were feeding a small child. This is her unconscious identification with her own mother who did not—and certainly in infant care, could not—respect the territory of her child. Furthermore, it expresses the almost automatic assumption of authority on the part of the woman. In other words, frequently without knowing that they do so, women extend limiting care to their husbands, thereby questioning their adulthood or adequacy. Since most men, because of their early developmental experiences, are prone to connect femininity with maternity, they are likely to regress in relation to their wives to a reaction level that would be more appropriate for a child rather than for an adult—namely, resentful compliance. In some ways men express the same tendency to infantilize their wives. In a society where both sexes are equally adept at driving a car, it can frequently be observed that men assume the driving as a matter of course when their wives are with them. They assume responsibility for drawing up a joint income tax return and for repair in house maintenance; they frequently assume the dominant position in intercourse as a "natural" position and consider themselves sophisticated when they agree or arrange to have the wife in the upper position.

Perhaps the most severe test of mature love in marriage is fidelity. It represents paying the price for the wish of not wanting to hurt the other. It means giving up new experiences, which most people crave, in order to protect the self-image of the other. Fidelity is willingness to carry the burden of untested fantasies for the sake of the spouse. Sacrificing fantasies for reality is the essence of fidelity. What is frequently overlooked is that such a burden becomes bearable only on a bedrock of satisfaction. Dissatisfied people will be likely to respond to every call of fantasy. In our time we have arranged for so many opportunities to increase our fantasies of commitment with new partners that the meaning of commitment is almost lost. We must then return to the question of whether the avoidance of the temptation of another relationship at the sacrifice of testing one's own fantasies can be expected in many marriages. Certainly, fidelity is unlikely if one has not received enough satisfaction in marriage to contemplate adultery with anticipatory guilt. It amounts to a decision as to whether the marriage is a prison or a setting of legitimate boundaries. Boundaries will be found legitimate when the territory which they surround is satisfactory. Thus, mutual satisfaction is still the best guardian of fidelity in marriage.

We live in a period which extols social change, is impatient with discomforts and irritations, and is inclined to sanction experimentations with refutation of traditional arrangements. Group marriages and marriage like arrangements of living together in commitment between people of the same sex are examples of this general tendency in the development of civilization. They are frequently supported by an ideology which considers progress as a condition of social well-being or is impatient with mere progress to the point where it demands revolution. Group marriages are also frequently an expression of obsolescence of the social roles which have been traditionally assigned to women, such as the roles of child rearer and homemaker or supervisor of the consumption aspect of family economics. For young women who are educated for a professional life or who see other women of their group so educated sitting in the suburbs with not enough to do, particularly after the children have gone to school, the situation of the role context of a housewife and mother may become increasingly intolerable and may suggest the arrangement of a group household. It is tempting for some to think that if, for instance, four families lived together in one house, only one of the four wives would assume household functions for a period of time and would set the others free for pursuit of self-realization either through occupations in the marketplace or through academic studies. These arrangements consider more what can be done with time gained than what can be lost in the giving up of dyadic experiences. In some ways they increase the temptation to engage in new marriages which is similar to the temptations that occur in the employment of women and men together. The closeness of living not only with one spouse but with a number of spouses who are married to other people produces the unavoidable development of positive or negative feelings toward these people. Where there are marital irritations, other people for whom positive relationships have been developed will suggest themselves as possible alternatives. When one is angry with one's husband and one has been comparing his behavior with the behavior of three other husbands that live in the same house or home community, what could be more understandable than to engage in fantasies that one or the other of these husbands might be a better partner? As a matter of fact, the closeness in group households may be more pronounced than the closeness of office contacts between men and women. The price to be paid for the release of time resulting from communal life is, therefore, the risk of being abandoned as well as the temptation of abandoning. It might also frequently be the case that the person to whom the home maintenance tasks are delegated may find himself or herself discriminated against and may perform these tasks resentfully and, therefore, inefficiently.

The marriagelike arrangements of homosexuals and lesbians seem to offer certain advantages. They free the partners from the risk of reproductive consequences of their intimacy; most of all, they free them from the difficulties of coping with difference and from the irritations which result. However, these characteristics are also disadvantages. We have pointed out that one of the greatest assets of a marriage is its developmental challenge for transition from adolescence to adulthood. In a "marriage" between persons of the same sex, there is usually no such developmental challenge because such a marriage omits the challenge of parenthood, of living in triadic and multiple relationships. Furthermore, it does not prevent irritations which follow from differences in temperament, differences in dominance, differences in congenital activity patterns, or differences resulting from developmental hazards. Incompatibility of defenses may still exist in childless people and will remain unmitigated by the prospect or reality of progeny. The problem of infidelity remains and will probably be aggravated by the absence of responsibility for children. Another problem with such experiments is their support by ideological considerations which may make it more difficult for the partners to admit that they have been failures than might be the case in traditional arrangements.

All reasonably adequate marriages are stages of transition in the life of the spouses. They share this characteristic with all other phases of the human experience which do not show rigidity and unadaptability to change. Marriage leads from singlehood to an end, either by divorce or by death. It has, therefore, the quality of pulling people away from familiar situations and presenting them with new challenges of adaptation.

Conceivably the most tragic outcome of the marital experience in relatively young couples is the unexpected death of a marriage partner. It is accepted that although marriages, by tradition, should come to an end in old age when one or the other partner dies, many young persons bring about termination of marriage by getting a divorce. However, people are still shocked when a young spouse is lost in war, in an accident, or through a premature terminal disease such as cancer. Survivorship is therefore not only a problem of old age. It occurs with sufficient frequency as a young marital experience to deserve attention in this context. As opposed to survivorship in advanced years, survivorship in a relatively young couple has an element of the unexpected and of unpreparedness. This experience again presents the familiar qualities of bipolarity—trauma and recovery. For some, the early death of a marriage partner has the element of inordinate loss. Something has been taken away which was expected to remain. People feel an element of injustice in such an occurrence. It is not seen as a natural event and cannot be integrated into the experience of the survivors as such.

Still, for some young people such a death opens up the advantage of returning to singlehood. If the survivor has become somewhat disenchanted with the deceased, it gives him or her a new range of choices, the possibility of pursuing self-fulfillment in intellectual or professional work or simply in the continuation of singlehood. The choices might also include the decision to marry again and involve the searching out of a new mate.

It might be postulated that an adequate marriage is a marriage which helps young adults to abandon the residues of adolescence, people in their middle life to maintain maturity, and people in their declining years to cope with the decline. It must prepare the partners for having to return to singlehood with little expectation of further dyadic or multiple relationships. In other words, it is ultimately a process of transition to yet another separation.

SUGGESTED READINGS

Nathan W. Ackerman, *The Psychodynamics of Family Life.* New York, Basic Books, 1958.
Robert R. Bell, *Marriage and Family Interaction.* Homewood, Ill., Dorsey Press, 1967.

Robert O. Blood, *Husbands and Wives.* New York, Free Press, 1965

Changing Sexual Values and the Family. G. Pirooz Sholevar, M.D., ed., Springfield, Ill., Charles C. Thomas, 1977

Divorce and After. P. Bohannon, ed., Garden City, N.Y., Doubleday & Co., 1970.

Richard A. Hunt and Edward J. Rydman, *Creative Marriage.* Boston, Holbrook Press, Inc., 1976.

M. Krantzler, *Creative Divorce,* New York. Evans & Co., 1973.

James Leslie McCary, *Freedom and Growth in Marriage.* Santa Barbara, Calif., Hamilton Publishing Company, 1975.

Clifford J. Sager, *Marriage Contracts and Couple Therapy.* New York, Brunner/Mazel, 1976.

Paul Watzlawick et al., *Pragmatics of Human Communication.* New York, W. W. Norton, 1967.

CHAPTER 11

Sons, Daughters, and Siblings-in-Law: Conflicting Loyalties

It is also part of the mythology of marital happiness that one marries only one person. In reality, one marries into the family in which one's spouse was a child. One acquires parents-in-law, brothers- and sisters-in-law, and conceivably even cousins-in-law. It should be noted at this point that this is the first phase of experience with in-law relationships. One becomes a son- or daughter-in-law, brother- or sister-in-law long before one becomes a mother- or father-in-law. Thinking in developmental terms, one might find here a parallel with the sequence of having to be a child before one becomes a parent. If there is malice generated through the limiting care which one experiences as a child, this malice is then unconsciously or even consciously expressed in the performance of one's role as a parent. One could equally assume that any malice which is generated by the conflicts in one's relationships with one's parents-in-law will later be consciously or unconsciously expressed when one becomes a father- or mother-in-law.

There is, however, an essential difference between the two experiences. When one is a child, parents and siblings are growth-enhancing and thus are functional. They are likely to be experienced as nurturers, protectors, models, or simply as auxiliaries in the process of growing up. The in-laws that one acquires upon marriage gain their status as parents and siblings when one is an adult and no longer needs any growth enhancement. It is frequently difficult enough for adults to have parents, brothers and sisters who cannot recognize this fact. How difficult must it be to double the situation?

When a woman gets married she frequently appears to her husband as he, in his unconscious, remembers his mother. The man will find in the woman he marries a woman such as his mother was, and roughly at an age that his mother had been when he was born. If, on top of this, she resembles his mother physically or psychologically, the husband may see in her the ideal spouse. He has everything: the image of his mother and a wife in the same person.

When one listens to wives talking about their mothers-in-law, one frequently gains the impression that many describe themselves. Over and beyond the similarity which must be present because she is of the same sex and is now probably at an age at which her mother-in-law was herself in the early years of marriage, there might be similarity in character. The description of mothers-in-law by their sons' wives, therefore, frequently reveals the mate selection dynamics of the husband. This is difficult to accept for women who have pronounced and conscious conflicts with their mothers-in-law. It might be more easily acceptable for those for whom the battle has not taken conscious and open forms.

The loyalty of every married male is divided between his mother and his wife. He feels that he has somehow to do right by two women. It is difficult enough to do right by one woman, but to do right by two women who may not like one another and have no reason to like one another, is an extraordinary and sometimes excruciating task.

Similar conflicts may exist for women in relation to father and husband but they do not seem to be so frequent, or at least do not seem to attract so much attention.

Although it is true to say that by marriage one acquires, as a rule, two more parents, and conceivably also siblings, by social assignment, this is not the complete story. Since the same happens to one's spouse, a marriage by definition presents to the young couple a problem of divided loyalties. Both the husband as well as the wife are likely to have in-laws with competitive claims for their attention, accommodation, and consideration. It is hard to sort out and honor these competitive claims on an equitable or at least conflict free basis.

One starts a second family with a tremendous pull-back of loyalty to the members of one's family of origin. This loyalty expresses itself first of all by the feeling that one should not have left them. If one can overcome that, one still feels that one should somehow preserve good relationships with them, and this is a source of repetitive discomfort in family life. Should one go to visit mother once a week, should one call mother once a day, should one have been over for Mother's Day and Father's Day, and Christmas and Hannukah and Thanksgiving? The problem of the family visit is always a problem of conflicting loyalties because it implies that at least one spouse will be where he or she doesn't want to be, or wouldn't be if it were not for the ties of marriage.

Perhaps most important, in-law trouble is felt as competition for the attention and commitment of the marriage partners. For most married people this presents a problem of painful decisions because what one gives to parents and brothers and sisters, one withholds from spouse and children, and what one gives the spouse and children, one takes from parents and brothers and sisters.

In this conflict-ridden situation, the family of origin has a number of strategic advantages. The in-laws were there first, they were there in the most formative years and they have the special tie of biological connection. Spouses and children come into one's life when parent and sibling relationships have long been formed. Every spouse is a latecomer compared with a parent. Even more so, he is a biological stranger and, for genetic reasons, preferably so. Unfortunately for marital harmony a stranger is seldom a match for a parent who does not want to let go.

One of the traditional ways of coping with family difficulties in our culture is avoidance by distancing. A young couple may deliberately settle in another part of the country. This coping pattern may have been developed well before the marriage when the young people went away to college. It is strengthened later on by the career mobility which has become part and parcel of American middle-class life. For those who cannot cope with divided loyalties by distancing—which is true especially among blue-collar families—patterns of accommodation have to be developed. For example, the couple might spend Christmas with one set of parents and Thanksgiving with another. This has two advantages. First, it removes the necessity of decision making on a holiday-by-holiday basis. Second, parents can count on being visited on these occasions and may derive from this a reassurance of relationship. Still, this arrangement has its drawbacks because telling one's parents about the accommodation that has been decided upon will document the experience of separation. Furthermore, no amount of routinization can conceal emotional preference for the house where one isn't considered a thief. A son-in-law may be welcome, whereas a daughter-in-law may not be because she has "stolen" her husband from his mother.

Children are frequently used by parents for some kind of satisfaction which they do not find in the marital relationship. This puts the children in a very unfair situation because they are powerless to resist the impact of this claim. There is probably something in heterosexual attraction, beyond its element of sexuality, which is related to the problem of incompleteness as against wholeness. The child-in-law of the opposite sex is an addition, completion, and the child-in-law of the opposite sex is an addition, a completion, and the child-in-law of the same sex corroborates the fractionalization of the human species and interferes with the wish for completion. In such cases, the completion wishes can become fulfilled only by grandchildren.

Perhaps less emphasis should be put on the frequency of in-law trouble (which is probably overstated because it is hardly ever compared with the frequency of marital or parent-child trouble) than on the nature of in-law troubles. In order to have some grasp on this aspect of the problem, the senior author asked a number of more mature students, ranging in age from the late twenties to the early fifties, to talk about their experiences with in-laws. Six students volunteered and gave sufficiently different stories to indicate that in-law relationships cover a wider range of persons and situations than is generally assumed.

One male student in the first year of his marriage claimed he had a very good relationship with his father- and mother-in-law. He described the relationship as close but without meddling on their part and gave two particular reasons for this satisfactory state of affairs. In the first year of his marriage he had been in the armed services and his wife had stayed with her parents but, due to her marriage, had been financially independent of them. This had provided a period of transition which had taken the sting out of the sudden separation which most parents suffer when children who have lived with them get married. Secondly, he and his wife had just become parents of a baby girl and this presented his in-laws with a much-longed-for granddaughter. It was fairly obvious that this report was given in a state of euphoria created by the arrival of the child, but it still contains significant features that we will find repeated in other instances where the in-law relationships seemed to present improvement or comfort. The separation created by the marriage had been softened by a period of transition and by the arrival of a grandchild of the longed-for sex.

The second student was a woman who reported that she was closer to her in-laws than her husband was to his but that they were basically very happy in their marriage. She added a significant point, however, in reporting that her husband had also not been very close to his parents, so that his relationship to his in-laws really replicated his relationship to his own parents. Here we have a phenomenon which will probably also be found in other cases, namely, the spillover of parent-child relationships into in-law relationships. It does not require much imagination to predict that people who have had good experiences with their parents are likely to expect and to elicit good experiences with their parents-in-law. Many human beings are monotonous and likely to repeat their experiences with earlier partners whenever a new life situation arises. One is almost tempted to say that if one wants to know how future spouses will relate to their in-laws, it might be helpful to look at how they related to their parents.

A third student reported in-law problems of long duration. She seemed to have been suffering from irritation and aggravation for a long time without finding an opportunity to express her accumulated grievances. When she started out by saying that she had a lot of in-law problems and was warned by the senior author not to say in public anything that she might later regret having said, she replied, "I won't regret it, I will love it; I can finally get back at them." One had the impression of an explosion of grievances. The gist of these grievances, however, was that her husband, the son of an economically successful and charming but, in family relationships, irresponsible man, had assumed the father role toward two of his brothers. He had helped one to earn a Ph.D. and let the other, with his family, live rent-free in a house which he had acquired for them. The third brother had not been a burden to her husband but, on the other hand, had not helped, either, in financing the higher education of one of the brothers or in alleviating the housing difficulties of the other. The woman felt that her own family had suffered by the diversion of funds and the tension created by her husband's care for his siblings. We have here a case of conflict with brothers-in-law rather than with the father- or mother-in-law, a phenomenon which is frequently overlooked and probably could be conceptualized also as a problem of divided loyalties and an indictment of a parent-in-law for not having done what he should have.

The fourth student said that he got along well with his in-laws but reported pressure for grandchildren to which he and his wife, both still pursuing academic studies, did not want to yield. He felt that the pressure would mount and be particularly difficult to meet because he and his wife were going to enter professions which would make having children much more difficult than in a traditional family supported by the earnings of one spouse.

The fifth student presented probably a more clinical picture than the preceding ones. She was divorced after two years of marriage and reported that the main reason for the breakup of her marriage had been the tendency of her mother-in-law to belittle her own son and to compare him unfavorably with her. Here the stereotype seems to be reversed. It is not the daughter-in-law with whom fault is found, but the son. On first impression, one cannot but wonder whether the mother-in-law did not unconsciously want to break up the marriage by creating tension between the marriage partners through making such a comparison. One could go a step further and hypothesize that the belittling of her own son was an attempt to convey the message that he was not ready for marriage and that the daughter-in-law could do better with someone else. Still going further in the analysis, one could even venture a guess that it was the student herself who had belittled her husband and had only projected upon her mother-in-law her own attitude toward her husband.

The sixth and last student to report in-law problems was a businesswoman well in her fifties who reported a thirty-year-long story of conflict with her father-in-law. She described him as someone who always had to be right, who knew the answers to all questions in business as well as all other areas. He had taken her husband into his business at the age of nineteen and she had joined the business soon after. Her father-in-law was still, in his retirement, going to the office daily and trying to call the signals, although the business had prospered under her and her husband far more than it had before.

In conclusion, these relationships add one more dynamic to a stage of life which is already very complex. They offer one more contradiction to the widespread assumption that married life can be easy.

SUGGESTED READINGS

T. Boszormenyi-Nagy and C. Spark, *Invisible Loyalties.* Hagerstown, Md. Harper & Row, 1973.

John L. Thomas, *The American Catholic Family.* Englewood Cliffs, N. J. Prentice Hall, 1956.

Willard Waller and Reuben Hill, *The Family: A Dynamic Interpretation.* New York, Dryden, 1951.

CHAPTER 12
Childlessness Versus Children

Perhaps two of the most outstanding characteristics of modern family life, at least in the urban middle class, is overwork of parents and the expensiveness of childrearing. In dual career marriages reproduction has a number of consequences which some people may be unwilling to accept. Having children is likely to delay the professional career of the wife so as to bring a feeling of injustice into their marriage. This feeling of injustice may be shared by husbands but it must be more deeply experienced by wives because it is they who have to carry the burden of pregnancy, to meet the demand of symbiotic life with the infant and to accept the concomitant interruptions of their studies or work, demands which their husbands do not have to meet.

Even when the mothers' careers are resumed, child care will probably make greater demands on mothers than on fathers. The specific biological tie between children and mother will frequently assert itself against social change. When children are sick, mothers are more likely to stay home than fathers and in sickness and health children seem to demand more attention from the mother than from the father. Mothers are, therefore, demanded to cover more positions than they can comfortably occupy. Career, household duties and childrearing produce an overload which is frequently accompanied by conflict. Whatever time is given to one seems to shortchange the other. Such situations frequently produce guilt no matter how time is distributed. They are likely to produce anger and failure in performance in one or the other area. Ultimately such constellations may produce a feeling that one is unable to cope, resulting in ineffectiveness, rage and depression.

Since the unique tie between mothers and children cannot be broken by whatever arrangements of role sharing the spouses may want to make, children present an unequal burden to the spouses in a dual career marriage. Bluntly, the wife will have three burdens and the husband will have two. At any rate biology will force working women to have interrupted careers or postpone careers for the same amount of education which will give husbands uninterrupted careers. A transfer of pregnancy to males unfortunately cannot be legislated.

Certainly at present, a pattern of equally sharing of the burdens of childrearing and household by husbands and wives seems not yet fully established and, for the reasons mentioned above, may not be possible to be established. Apparently the demands which children make on the mothers are oblivious of the desirabilities of social change.

It need not surprise, therefore, that numbers of young women decide to remain childless and that their husbands agree with them. Such agreements are usually a source of conflict with their parents who wish grandchildren in their own desire for a bridge to immortality. This is an egotistical pressure because the pleasures of grandparenthood would have to be paid for by career disruption of the wife and, conceivably, also of her husband. At any rate, the burdens and the conflict of childrearing would have to be borne by sons and daughters and not by their parents. It has also to be considered that college educated people expect parenting to be difficult and ultimately unrewarding because of the widespread suspicion that effective parenting is an infrequent ability. Parents and particularly mothers are always under the latent indictment of having caused the difficulties of their children. It is understandable that some people consider the possibility that their children may be the cause of difficulties which could be avoided by childlessness.

Formerly, and particularly in rural areas, children were economic assets. They could contribute cheap labor to the running of a farm, they could help the mother in household duties or even with the rearing of younger children. Today they seem to be expensive burdens without any near future expectation of reward. It is true that in old age one may regret not having had children to lean on but old age is hardly ever a factor in planning for the near future.

Frequently people take a middle position regarding the problem of having children or not having children. They postpone the decision until they become anxious that childbirth may become too difficult for the wife and find out that it does not become difficult but impossible. It could also be that people who decide to remain childless have a suspicion that they cannot have children and do not want to admit to themselves that their childlessness is deficit rather than choice. It is, of course, possible to find out whether one can have children or not but it may be more comfortable not to have certainty in this matter. In a society which still expects a marriage to lead to children, it is easier to convey to others the idea that one is postponing childbearing rather than the idea that one does not want any children.

From an existentialist point of view, the decision to remain childless is, of course, renunciation of a human potential but, at least for women, the decision to have children is also renunciation, the renunciation of an uninterrupted career. Unless child care institutions would be so developed that parenting would be reduced to a tolerable minimum without damage to the child, we might expect more and more couples to decide in favor of child-lessness.

It must also be considered that we are living in a society in which, practically, one out of two marriages will end in divorce. This will mean, of course, that people are getting married consider-ing the possibility that their marriage will end in divorce and that they may not want to expose children to the conflict and suffering which divorce usually means for them. In practical terms and in ethical terms it is much easier to decide on a divorce when children are not involved. It also increases the chance of the spouses to be considered as partners for remarriage. Courageous must be the man who would marry a woman with five children, courageous the wife who would want to marry a father already burdened with heavy support expenses for children from a first marriage. Another aspect of childless marriage is the fact that the growth of children does not remind one of one's own age. It provides an almost magic atmosphere of timelessness until the unavoidable reminders of mortality break the charm.

In view of all these considerations, one is forced to the conclusion that a dual career marriage can be truly egalitarian only if it remains childless. Only the future can tell how many people will realize this—to many—unacceptable truth.

SUGGESTED READINGS

Robert O. Blood, Jr. and Donald M. Wolfe, *Husbands and Wives, The Dynamics of Married Living*. New York, The Free Press, 1960.

Lucille Duberman, *Marriage and its Alternatives*. New York, Praeger Publishers, Inc., 1974.

William F. Kenkel, *The Family in Perspective*. Third Ed., Pacific Palisades, California, Goodyear Publishing Company, Inc., 1973.

Arlene Skolnick, *The Intimate Environment, Exploring Marriage and the Family*. Boston, Little, Brown and Company, 1973.

CHAPTER 13

Parenthood: The Conservation of Adulthood Under Attack

Up to now we have discussed the experience of living from the child's point of view. This seems to be in harmony with the general tenor of discussions of child development. Research, scholarship, and popular writing seem to be done by children's advocates. From this point of view, the parents by definition seem to be under permanent indictment for causing developmental failures in their children. Successful child rearing is not discussed as an occurrence which happens spontaneously but as a desirable skill that has to be taught in family-life education and in parent-effectiveness training. In this chapter we will make an attempt to discuss child rearing from the parent's point of view.

We want to introduce a new perspective on the developmental experience in family life by identifying an element of parenthood that usually remains unmentioned. An adult person gains not only a host of new functions and burdens by having children, but also a new status and an often denied power over their children. As has been mentioned in the previous chapter, reproduction is socially expected from married people and adults who are childless, whether voluntarily or involuntarily, are frequently considered to be somehow deficient and unfulfilled. In order to enjoy the status of parenthood, then, one must have children. This observation may appear trite, but it is not so when one considers that a person does not gain the status of being a child by having parents. One can be an orphan or one can be separated from one's parents by social upheaval, but one would still have the privileges and the developmental burdens of being a child. A person who has remained childless is somebody who has never gained parenthood and its accompanying status. This, however, is an experience which expresses perhaps more strongly than any other the bipolarity of life.

We believe that adulthood implies a number of tests, the most demanding of which is parenthood. The test essentially requires the development of two capabilities. The first is the power to perform the function of parenting as long as it is needed. The second, which we will discuss in the following chapter, is the ability to abandon one's parental function when it is no longer needed by adult sons and daughters.

In our opinion, it is a fallacy to discuss parenthood only in terms of what children receive from their parents. It would seem to us more appropriate to discuss parenthood in terms of what parents gain from their children and what they have to give up or are at the risk of losing.

Having pointed out the socially valued status of parenthood, we must now turn to its price. Parenthood is first of all the giving up of the comforts and ease of dyadic living with another adult. One has to share the marriage partner with a child or children. One must permit and share his or her response to immature demands. One has to give of oneself to a new source of trouble and worries. One has to give up the relative ease of divorce and the relative ease of remarriage of the childless. It is probably more important in developmental terms that parenthood is a responsibility which in itself tests the power of human beings to give, to be effective in giving, and to be accountable to other social institutions, such as school and health care, for the maturation and the intellectual and emotional development of their sons and daughters. This responsibility requires the development of capabilities such as the courage to recover from reversals, and the ability to withstand the stimulation of regression which the impulse-directed life of small children presents to the person who assumes a child care task. The demands of responsibility and the stimulation of regression combine therefore to test the adulthood of the parent.

The discussion of parenthood from the viewpoint of the child has led to a pervasive attitude on the part of most people to keep parents under continuous accusation for having failed their children in helping their development. We would like to present another perspective, namely, that the responsibility and the regressive stimulation of childcare and child rearing may provide a stimulus for further development for parents and not only a test of their capabilities. To have brought up a child or children may be considered a success story as well as a story of failure. To invest in a child as much giving as is usually required without being rewarded by some feeling of achievement and personal growth would probably be a source of unhappiness which borders on the intolerable. It is unfortunate that only people who do not attain these rewards from parenting seem to furnish the data for the analysis of family dynamics.

It is, of course, true that, as with all tests, the test of parenthood will be failed by some. But it is probably one of the greatest unintended consequences of clinical discussions of parenthood that the history of failure is being written as the history of parenthood and that the history of success remains unrecorded and parents are denied the homage that they deserve. One could say that parenting is an opportunity to show one's adulthood as well as a test of one's adulthood. Those who either show that they have the capacity to use the opportunity, or who develop the capacity because of the demands of the opportunity of which they have availed themselves need to be brought to attention.

We have had occasion in earlier parts of this book to point out that the exchanges in family life cannot be evaluated in terms of the criterion of who gets more. Instead, the criterion should emphasize who can give more without having to get what he considers in egotistical terms to be a full return. Although the exchange principle between parents and children is probably pervasive, we might, in spite of our insistence that child rearing must bring rewards, consider it another test of maturity to be able to give more than one receives. We consider a parent who wants to get from the children as much satisfaction as he or she gives to them as immature, as having failed at least one test of adulthood. Such a parent may want to continue to get satisfactions even when the exchanges have stopped because the child has become an independent self-servicing and self-directing person.

Seen from another perspective, we would like to suggest also that tests of adulthood which parenthood does present can be failed because of the kind of behavior which has been identified in transactional analysis. When adults treat other adults as children or as parents, the transaction is likely to fail. It will fail particularly if one person accepts such inappropriate treatment by the other. When spouses accept being parented by their spouses they may have an emotionally satisfactory interaction, but they have lost their adulthood. Even worse, when parents expect parenting from their children, family pathology is likely to be acute and in many instances even extreme. It should not be overlooked, however, that many adults are inviting other people not to treat them as adults. The erroneous fantasy of more comfortable periods in one's childhood will probably seduce many people into evoking parenting in people who are not their parents. This does not apply only to spouses; it applies to employers, teachers, friends, and conceivably therapists. Another form of transactional failure is what we would like to call the "spousing" of children. This is usually referred to as "incest" and it may be a more frequent occurrence than is publicly known because incest is one of the intensely kept family secrets. Parents who are stimulated by the physical maturation of their adolescent sons and daughters into reacting to the revival of the oedipal situation with positive response, rather than with rejection, also fail the test of adulthood. We might, therefore, conclude that adolescents are testing, consciously or unconsciously, the adulthood of their parents. It is the proof of adulthood to pass this test by insistence on separation instead of yielding symbolically or factually to the oedipal invitation.

The complexities of parenting have been paradoxically increased by an attempt to simplify them. Over the last fifty years, parents—particularly mothers—have gradually delegated many of their functions to child-care professionals. They have not shown, however, any inclination to give up the status and the power that go with parenthood. Routinely, they resume both parental status and function when the children come home. This, at best, is complicated by problems of synchronization.

Although children's services have virtually always been designed to liberate mothers from the twenty-four-hour assignment of child care, it should be noted that child care institutions, and, later, the school system, have not synchronized their schedules with the working schedules of mothers who have entered the labor market. It is true that a working mother may be able to bring her child to a day care center and then go on to her place of work or study, but her working or study time will be cramped by the need to get the child back from the day care center at an hour earlier than would be feasible for her. If the father takes over the fetching of the child, the same bind may apply to him. Men's work and study schedules also are not synchronized with the schedules of day care centers, nursery schools, kindergarten, and the general school system. It should be stated that in terms of time, job and studies are more demanding than child care institutions. A child is not kept by such an institution beyond, say, seven hours. The normal working day in our society is still eight. We are here faced with a cultural lag which has remained remarkably free from remedial attention.

Even if a synchronization between institutionalized child care and study or work time should be ultimately achieved, we would still have to face the problem that a child would probably be reunited with a tired parent. We have always been doubtful about the mythology of the kibbutz according to which parents who have worked hard in the fields all day come home "to enjoy two hours" with their children before the children are returned to the children's house. The fact that many children raised in kibbutz child care arrangements leave the kibbutz when they get married testifies to the potential validity of our doubt.

For the time being, at any rate, working women have to make arrangements between institutional child care or school closing time and their arrival at home. This presents an additional pressure for them. It requires more decision making, more arrangements, and actually presents a new specific parental burden formerly not known.

From the point of view of comparative institutional analysis, we find what we have found before and are probably going to find again, that other institutions impose their standards on the institution of the family. The same is true for the health care system which schedules clinic hours without regard for the demands which a mother has to meet during those hours. There is also the tendency of the school system to blame family disturbances for learning disabilities of children and to enforce family treatment where a teacher does not succeed in fulfilling his own task. In view of all this one might wish to see assertiveness training extended to fighting the submission of family life to the organizational ease of other institutions.

SUGGESTED READINGS

John Bowlby, *Attachment.* New York, Basic Books, 1969.
Sylvia Brody, *Patterns of Mothering.* New York. International Universities Press, 1956.
Thomas Gordon, *Parent Effectiveness Training.* New York, Wyden, 1970.
Franz Kafka, *Letter to His Father* (Translated by E. Kaiser and E. Wilkins) New York, Schocke, 1966.
Alexander Mitscherlich, *Society Without the Father.* New York, Harcourt, Brace & World, 1963.
D. W. Winnicott, *The Maturational Processes and the Facilitating Environment: Studies in the Theory of Emotional Development.* London, Hogarth Press, 1965.
Parenthood: Its Psychology and Psychopathology. E. J. Anthony and T. Benedek, eds., Boston, Little, Brown and Co., 1970.

PART IV

Selfishness versus Selflessness in a
Losing Battle

CHAPTER 14

A New Dyad: The Home without Children

In families with children there comes a time when their parents realize that the last child has left the home to establish an independent lifestyle. This realization is usually accompanied by a transitional period of "mourning" in which the parents have a feeling of loss. At first they cannot accept the loss and may respond to it with anger or depression, but ultimately they adapt to it. We have tried to indicate throughout this book that life in the family presents a series of adaptations which become increasingly burdensome as life goes on because earlier adaptations fight the willingness to try new ones. The difficulty which underlies many of the new adaptations the couple is required to make during this period involves abandoning their function as parents.

As we have implied before, parenthood is a status derived from having reproduced. While this status is accompanied by life-maintaining and life-enhancing functions during the first two decades of a child's life, these functions are lost when the child reaches adulthood and no longer needs parental care. However, since the status of parenthood remains after these two decades, it represents at least a temptation to have it accompanied by the continuation of earlier parental functions.

Adulthood, in our definition, is the experience of being able to give more than one gets and the experience of letting go when one's giving is no longer required. In some way, resistance on the part of parents to accept aging as an unavoidable phenomenon in the developmental process makes them increasingly unable to discontinue the self- and socially-imposed presumption of parenthood. Since one cannot let go without replacement of the life content that one has had to release, adulthood after loss of functional parenthood requires new fulfillments. This is a problem which is experienced less frequently by males because their parenting has been accompanied traditionally by another type of life content, namely, that of a provider. It is particularly a problem for females whose life content in the past has been determined by maternity. We project that mothers in the future will find it easier to cease their attempts to maintain parental influence over their adult sons and daughters. They will either have built up work or interests while their children grew up or will take up such alternate self-fulfillments after the children have left the home.

The necessity of abandoning the parental function at the appropriate time is the essence of the new dyadic experience in which the spouses find themselves in an "empty nest." They must find substitute satisfaction either in the renewal of the old dyadic relationship or in new types of relationships which are probably more adaptive but are under the shadow of the implications of declining years. The implications are, first, the feeling that one has passed the peak of life, and second, that one is approaching the difficulties of retirement, loneliness and, possibly, terminal disease. This time of life therefore ideally requires more courage than earlier periods when adaptations were supported by optimism about the future.

The adaptations which a couple in this phase of life have to make are related to space and time. It is probably wise for people whose children cannot be expected to come home regularly, even if it were only for visits, to reduce the space of their housing arrangement. It is undoubtedly adaptive to exchange a house which was supposed to shelter sons and daughters for a house which has the function of sheltering only the spouses. This implies in some ways an admission of narrowing life space and is, therefore, a difficult though appropriate adaptation. It has, however, its rewards in bringing about harmony between domestic demands and the declining vitality of persons who have to live without help. The wish for permanence of one's home is therefore increasingly maladaptive at this period of life.

For people who do not believe in a life after death, the consideration of declining capacities and time produces the challenge of catching up with apparent opportunities that were missed and of compensating for satisfactions that were lost. The activation of decision making by a limitation of time is frequently stronger than the realization of limited opportunities. This raises the interesting question of whether the ability to change which we have stated to be a principle of health can be evaluated without any realistic consideration of the possible consequences of initiating such changes. The limitation of time gives fewer chances to correct mistakes, to use the lessons of trial and error, and to attain the degree of competence which earlier learning has produced. It would seem to be, therefore, one of the tasks of a couple whose children have left to protect one another from erratic and unrealistic changes of lifestyle.

A positive self-image can be battered by the new experience of partial failure. We think that it is an important function of older marriage partners to help one another to reach appropriate self-acceptance. Forgetting of names, greater fatigue, increasing irritability, sleeplessness at night and sleepiness during the daytime are failings that one must learn to permit oneself in advancing years. To find tolerance for such changes in the other is frequently one of the rewards of maintaining one's marriage and is unlikely to be found in a new marital relationship.

In spite of the somewhat somber picture that we have drawn so far of this phase of marriage, we must add that there are also certain advantages for the new dyadic experiences of the aging couple which were not available earlier. In many cases the new dyadic experience will begin after the spouses have had more time available to them to reduce their strangeness to one another through mutual adaptations and a corresponding renunciation of egotistical idiosyncrasies. If not that, they may have learned to live with strangeness, so that it no longer bothers them as much as before or makes them feel that the demands they made on their marriage have not been met. Perhaps most significant, long years of living together have produced a familiarity with the adulthood of the other which makes the need to know about the other's life before the marriage less intense, if such a need continues at all. Now the time passed together is longer than the time passed in singlehood, and the relationship gains relevance and legitimacy from this mere fact.

It is frequently overlooked that old relationships have one advantage over new relationships. People who have become involved with one another when they were young have a perceptual preservative built into their relationship. People who have been married to one another twenty-five years or more will appear younger to one another than to anybody else. People are essentially building later stimuli into an earlier perceptive mass which is a defense against the inroads of time. Having been young together is something which no new encounter can provide. The maintenance of early relationships is therefore a defense against the perception of aging. A second marriage with an age-appropriate partner must start and proceed without the sheen of radiant youth which a first marriage provides. Marriage counselors who work for the preservation of aging marriages have, therefore, the earlier perceptions on their side.

Of course, the passage of time and the perspective of diminishing time increases anxiety about fulfilling fantasies that so far have not been fulfilled. A marriage at this stage is frequently disturbed by temptations which have existed earlier but which now seem to become activated by the prospect of termination. At this juncture, marriages therefore run a certain risk of being split up in the pursuit of unfulfilled fantasies going back for a long period of time. Since these fantasies have lasted so long, they are likely to be about a youthful partner. One sometimes learns that an old man has divorced his wife and has married a younger woman. There is always a suspicion that such a woman has made a calculating marriage decision guided by financial or prestige considerations rather than affection. Such marriages, of course, are frequently unsatisfactory because friction with the man's middle-aged sons or daughters or his physical failings and deterioration are likely to disappoint the young woman in her expectations.

In the late phase of the marriage the wife is likely to be beyond childbearing age. The spouses engage therefore in nonreproductive sex but not by choice as it might have been before. This fact could make one either mourn or enjoy liberation from former burdens: it liberates the couple from the burden of anxiety about unwanted parenthood, from the need to use contraceptives, and from the interruptions dictated by the menstrual cycle. One could say, therefore, that sex in this period is likely to be sex without fear and without restrictions. But we again find bipolarity in this situation. If it is sex without fear, it is also sex without hope. If it is sex without a structure determined by physiology, it may have to be sex restructured by psychological preferences.

In this phase the spouses, but particularly the wife, have had such a long period of giving behind them that they may well be exhausted and unwilling to continue their giving or to direct it to the other. Mothers, particularly, may have felt that their life has been an incessant series of giving to their husband and children and may feel that it is time for a cessation. The husband may, therefore, face a nongiving wife and find legitimation in the pursuit of his fantasies. As in all other instances of marital experience, we find it difficult to believe that in any marital difficulty, only one partner is the determining factor. This is a situation where our persistent concern with the interplay between egotism and altruism comes into play. People who are exhausted by living or exhausted by giving are tempted to close their systems and to feed upon themselves rather than upon others, particularly if the other has stopped his willingness to do the feeding. This may be adaptive in view of the impending separation of the couple by terminal disease and, ultimately, death. It is, however, very difficult for people to restrict their emotional involvement simply because of impending separation. In other words, the closing of the system will probably be a reaction to the past and not a preparation for the future.

So far we have only considered the probability that the wife and mother will have had the burden of giving in a marriage and parenthood and may therefore feel that she is through with giving. It could be, however, that two dependent people have married one another, each expecting the other to give without much concern about his or her own responsibility to give. They may have succeeded in the marriage because they had enough adulthood to acknowledge their need to give to children and may have been able to accomplish that part of familial giving. When the children have left they might find themselves facing the fact that they do not have anything to give to one another and have been disappointed in what they expected to receive. Such realizations are likely to lead to divorce after the children are gone.

A third possibility for the ending of long-established marriages is that an infrequently acknowledged stimulant for sex between the parents has disappeared, namely, their children. Children represent two types of sexual stimulants to their parents. When they are small, their relatively free impulse life, or, in Freudian terminology, the infantile perversions which they exhibit, may stimulate the return of the repressed in their parents. In other words, it may bring infantile sensual or sexual wishes in masked form back into the preconscious or conscious of the parents, create anxieties and drive them into the defense of marital sublimation. What appears as a satisfactory sex life may be a flight into adult heterosexuality. As the children approach adulthood, the sexual stimulus which they represent to the parent of the other sex may well become less masked and, therefore, much more anxiety-creating and the new conscious flight from incestuous temptation might keep the marital sex life going. When these stimuli disappear, the sex life of the parents may lose the fuel of activation which the children have represented and may come to an end. A marriage without sex tends to encompass a narrower experiential range and, by this very restriction, prepares the partners for the separation experience of survivorship. It may also do so to a degree in the emotional dimension. Lack or slowing down of sexual response may be interpreted by one or the other of the spouses as loss of love and thus cause heartache or hostility.

SUGGESTED READINGS

Simone de Beauvoir, *The Coming of Age*. New York, G. P. Putnam's Sons, 1972.

R. N. Butler and M. I. Lewis. *Aging and Mental Health: Positive Psychosocial Approaches*. St. Louis, Mo., C. V. Mosby, 1973

CHAPTER 15

The Mother-in-Law: The Ridiculed Tragedy

Usually connected with the experience of the new dyad is the experience of being a parent-in-law. This by its very nature offers a temptation to compensate inordinately for the newly experienced loneliness and yet another separation in the course of developmental change. It tempts people to violate the parental obligation of letting go. The capability of giving up parenting is most severely tested when children get married. Although this involves both spouses, it is usually the mother-in-law who is singled out as a problem in-law, as the person who makes trouble in the marriage of her children because she refuses to let go. She is frequently made the butt of jokes and the target of the hostility of sons and daughters who find it difficult to be claimed as children at a time when they are appropriately claimed as husbands or wives by their spouses. At any rate, there are no father-in-law jokes and this suggests that fathers-in-law do not present such difficulties to their children and their marriage partners as their wives do.

Since humor usually is a defense which conceals a painful truth, we should like to present the mother-in-law not as a ridiculous person but as a tragic figure who cannot help her own suffering and cannot help causing suffering to her own sons or daughters and their spouses. By this time her children are married and her own parents have either died or are under the shadow of death. She is thrown back upon her husband as the major anchor in her life but he, by definition, has remained a stranger in comparison with her parents. Even if she should have succeeded in reducing the strangeness of her spouse to a minimum, she is now saddled with a new stranger, the son- or daughter-in-law. If several of her children have married, her life may become crowded with strangers.

Ultimately, every child is experienced by the mother as her product because during the gestation period her child was literally part of her. After the first year of the childrearing period, she has had to reduce her closeness with her child more and more. When the "child" marries, she is expected to give up this product and suffer her son or daughter to have a union with someone else. To heap injustice on injury, society expects the mother to enjoy this. To her, however, it seems an incredible imposition to have brought a human being from the moment of birth to the point of adulthood and then to have to give him or her to another person. It is difficult to see that any mother in her heart can do this very graciously. Some of the crying at weddings is probably not joyful but mournful. For the mother, the whole idea of a wedding ceremony has an element of denial. The mother tries to believe that what happens does not occur, namely, a sorrowful parting. The mourning is turned into rejoicing but it has an element of untruth in it. She must cope with the experience of the return to "the empty nest," as we mentioned earlier. There is loneliness after the wedding; somebody who was there is not there anymore; so it must be cause for mourning, since one always mourns losses. Young people who elope actually show an element of sensitivity in refusing the denial ceremony.

There is, however, a range of possible rewards for this experience of loss. There is the potential of biological perpetuation through grandchildren, and many people hold great store by that fact, for it promises the continuation of part of oneself after death. It also shows other people that one has not produced an unmarrying or unmarriageable child, which implies parental failure. In some ways, therefore, the in-law experience seems to be a double-bind experience. Society bids parents and especially women to prepare children for marriage. However, their own feelings tell them that this is an unfair demand.

Theoretically, there should be familial rewards. The mother-in-law would let her son go but would gain a daughter-in-law. The father-in-law would let a daughter go and would gain a son-in-law. If parents cannot see the situation in this light, they find it difficult to let their children go. It is likely to be more difficult for a mother than for a father because ultimately a mother must let go of part of herself, while fathers never experience children biologically as part of themselves. Although a mother loses part of herself in the marriage of every child of hers, when her son marries she loses the sense of completion or the experience of having attained wholeness through him. If her daughter marries she still loses a part of herself but she gains the experience of symbolic heterosexual completion through acquiring a son-in-law. The father-in-law does not feel that he loses part of himself. If he loses a son, he gains a daughter-in-law and thus experiences a new "romance." If he loses a daughter, he loses only a "romance" and he may gain a son.

The essence of the mother-in-law experience is well summarized in the saying that when your son marries you lose him, but when your daughter marries you gain a son. This apprehension about loss expresses itself in the frequent tendency of mothers to disapprove of the mate selection of their sons. This is likely to be a rationalization of the fact that mothers really do not want their sons to get married at all. Therefore, no daughter-in-law will do. It is more acceptable, however, to say that it is only particular ones that will not do. This psychology of the mother-in-law is deeply rooted in biology and is particularly trying in modern times. In times when parents arranged the marriages of their sons and daughters, mothers could at least experience a certain influence on the mate selection of their children. They may have done so reluctantly but they responded to social expectation and enjoyed the rewards of a measure of power in the decision. Today sons and daughters marry those they have selected themselves or those who have selected them. In either case, the mother does not even have the consolation of having had a part in the decision making that resulted in the marriage. Even worse, many mothers-in-law have to come to terms not only with one daughter-in-law but with two or three daughters-in-law who have successively married their son. In a divorce-ridden society such as ours, the difficulties that the mother-in-law experiences are likely to be repetitious.

Trying to understand the root of the in-law trouble as a generic form of human development, we must again dwell on the problem of separation. In our society, most marriages imply that a child leaves his parents and takes up living with a child of other parents. Thus, the majority of marriages are preconditioned on the loss of children by two couples. The pressure for grandchildren that is so widely reported seems to be the major compensation which in-laws can expect for their loss.

SUGGESTED READING

Bob and Margaret Blood, *Marriage*. Third ed., New York, The Free Press, 1978.

Evelyn M. Duvall, *In-Laws: Pro and Con*. New York, Association Press, 1954.

Paul C. Glick, *American Families*, New York, Wiley, 1957.

Hope Jensen Leichter and William E. Mitchell, *Kinship and Casework*, New York, Russell Sage Foundation, 1967.

CHAPTER 16

Survivorship: Fighting the End without Support

Although this may change in the future, it must still be said that survivorship in a marriage is more frequently the fate of women than of men. This may be due to the fact that under traditional arrangements women married older men. It may also be due to the fact that the exertions and tribulations of earning a living made higher demands on the male body than the traditional feminine roles did on the female body. It could simply be a result of the physiological superiority of women over men. Whatever the reason, the widow is a more common phenomenon in our time than the widower. What one might also assume is that women have developed more of a traditional pattern of coping with the loss of a husband than men have with the loss of a wife. If health permits, women can continue the traditional role of homemaker for them-selves, although the task may become more burdensome if it is performed without male help. Men who have resisted the ex-changeability of roles which modern life has brought about will find the task of homemaking for themselves a novel necessity when their wives have died and will have to meet this challenge without preparation. Husbands of liberated women, on the other hand, will be better prepared to assume this function as their total responsi-bility. One might therefore venture a guess, that, at least in this respect, modern middle-class life prepares men better for being the survivors in the marriage than more traditional arrangements used to do.

The essence of the loss of a spouse, however, is the experience of aloneness after having not been alone. To a degree, this represents a repetition of singlehood. However, it is different from the singlehood experience of young people in that it is experienced at the decline of the life cycle and under the shadow of death. It is not a preparatory stage in life; it represents the closing stage. The aloneness of survivorship is also different from the loneliness after a divorce because death is final and one cannot harbor the hope that one's spouse may one day return.

Although it may sound shocking, one must concede that every loss, even the loss of a beloved spouse, represents a measure of liberation and thus, after the mourning passes, fantasies of replacement will be stimulated. Such a replacement, however, will be difficult because objects last longer than people and the possessions, such as clothes, bed or favorite chair, which have become associated with the deceased spouse will serve as constant reminders of the departed and will make the introduction of a new person into this life sphere seem like a violation of loyalty.

As has been the case with people whose children have left the home, the house in which the spouses have lived is likely to be too large for the survivor. It is likely to be too large in two ways. One person does not need as much space as two people and one person cannot handle the maintenance of that space as well as two.

The survivor is also thrown into celibacy again, a condition of existence with which he may have lost familiarity for the better part of his life. This celibacy is almost by definition prolonged because society expects a period of mourning and regards as a deviant anyone who wishes to shorten this period of celibacy and loneliness by entering into a new union.

People who exert this social pressure, especially adult sons and daughters, tend to overlook the fact that survivors are usually old people and have not much time left in which to find a new partner, to overcome the the strangeness which living with a new partner implies, and to make the necessary adjustments which every attempt to live in closeness with a new person requires. One year is not much for a young person; for an old person, it may be the rest of his life. Beggars for time can ill afford to be patient mourners.

There is therefore an unconscious cruelty in the social demand for mourning if it is made without consideration for the age of the mourner. It bids him not to look, and if he has looked, to behave as if he had not found.

The celibacy period is also physiologically harder for males than for females because non-use produces glandular atrophy of the prostate and changes socially demanded abstinence into a physical disability. For women the ending of sex relations may often be more an emotional loss than a physical one. They are likely to have passed the menopause when they become widows, and any trauma connected with glandular change is likely to have occurred before the loss of the spouse.

At any rate, it is quite possible that the absence of sexual demands that existed before may make life easier for some survivors; others again may enjoy, or suffer under, a regression to masturbation. Other forms of "adolescent" behavior may emerge as coping mechanisms in this stage. The survivor may begin socializing with a peer group of his or her own sex. This represents an attempt to return to a stage in which the company of people of one's own sex represented security, although it was the security created by an avoidance of the risk of failure in heterosexual relations.

Some people at this stage of life may want to join the families created by their children's marriages or the households of children who have chosen singlehood. Widowed parents frequently profess that they wish to preserve their independence, that they do not want to burden their children, and that they want to continue living alone. Even if they do so, they count on the availability of their grown-up sons and daughters to take care of them in sickness and distress. They frequently show their suffering and, in one form or another, return to the dependency of childhood and make the claims that children make on their parents. They sometimes exercise these dependency claims with petulance and become problem members of the families of their adult sons and daughters. Even if they handle their aloneness as the ultimate test of separation with dignity and without becoming a burden on others, their life represents a closing of the system. When there is nobody left from whom to receive nurture, one must nurture oneself.

Ideally, the survivor should be thankful that the deceased spouse has not had to suffer the sorrow and trauma of being the survivor. Realistically, however, the survivor may explicity or implicity complain, "Why am I the one to be left alone?" A factor that may add to this more selfish but sometimes inevitable reaction is the development of a belief in the other's irreplaceability. If one or both spouses have developed this belief, they will not prepare for survivorship by increasing and cultivating their social network. Furthermore, in most instances one cannot prepare for the emotional reaction to a spouse's death because this would require emotional distancing while he or she is still alive. In short, preparation for a spouse's death is always a most difficult task. Only in cases of terminal disease is anticipatory mourning possible because the difficulties of the last months make death appear as a release for the departed as well as for the survivor.

One can, however, prepare for the practical and economic aspects of survivorship, such as how to spend one's time and how to survive alone financially. This is traditionally an area of living in which many husbands fail their wives. Having assumed responsibility for the financial arrangements of the family, they leave their wives without information and experience as to how to handle income and investment, how to prepare income tax returns, and how to budget with the prospect of an income that decreases in purchasing power. Needless to say, it is likely that this will also change when more women will have had the experience of earning money and managing finances.

In summary, one could say that the better one has learned to cope with previous separations in one's life, the better one will be able to adjust to the ultimate separation from one's spouse. For many people, spending the last years alone is appropriate for their particular temperament, as well as a realistic assessment of their situation. Of course for some it may be simply the result of inertia.

Unfortunately, the period of survivorship may be spent considering alternatives to aloneness and experimenting with them. The first alternative that usually comes to mind is a second marriage, but such an experiment is beset with difficulties. Survivors will frequently not settle for an age-appropriate partner. They will try to repeat their first marriage in which they married someone who was young and, in their perception, stayed young. When an old person, however, makes an age-appropriate second marriage, there is no youth to be perceptually preserved. The recall of one's departed spouse as a relatively youthful person represents therefore, an unfair handicap for the new spouse, who will be compared with a much younger person in the perceptual delusions of the survivor.

There is also an element of exploitation in the remarriage of older persons. Older women may find themselves at a disadvantage here because they have lost the physical attractiveness to which men most frequently respond in making a marriage decision. They are therefore likely to be married not for their basic femaleness but for their money or simply for the relief of loneliness which they may be able to provide. Older men, in contrast, may be at an advantage because they have fewer competitors and may have prestige which appeals to potential partners. They, too, however, run the risk of being married not for themselves but for their money or for the company they promise to provide. In any case, a second marriage can provide at best only a few years of an acceptable life which will have to be paid for with the same discomforts of the terminal stage for partners who have not had time to accumulate the readiness for sacrifice and suffering provided by a lifelong marriage.

Still, there may be an element of altruism in "September-May" marriages. The younger spouse may wish only to have a platonic relationship which can satisfy certain needs, and the older spouse may find a suitable "child" to take care of him. Physiological or psychological reasons may make it easy not to insist on sexual union in such a relationship. One advantage which these marriages between young and old have over remarriage between two old people is the marriageability of the person who is likely to survive which may spare her the pains of prolonged or permanent survivorship.

An institutionalized form of regression for survivors is entrance into an old-age home which, by and large, is found unsatisfactory by the survivors and their sons and daughters. It symbolizes the last step before the death of the survivor, it diminishes him or her socially and psychologically, it fills the children with guilt about not having taken their parent into their own homes, and it is expensive.

The means of combating loneliness without the difficulties of a second marriage or of entering an old-age home is one which has been widespread but not freely admitted. This is change of consciousness through the use of alcohol, tranquilizers and pain-killers. Many survivors live and die in a state of chemically induced euphoria. It should be stated in this context that there is a vast difference between the drug abuse and alcoholism in the young and those in the old. For the young it is an arrest of potential; for the old it may be a pleasant bridge into nothingness. Philosophically and morally speaking, however, it is a choice between painful heroism and painless cowardice. It should also be noted that at least in the terminal stages in a hospital, painless cowardice is institutionally supported because a dying patient is much less trouble to the staff if he is under sedation than if he is facing death with a clear mind. At any rate, it is not only useless but probably cruel to react negatively to the choice of coping methods by a survivor in his loneliness and essentially hopeless situation.

SUGGESTED READINGS

Lynn Caine, *Widow.* New York, Morrow, 1974.

Elaine Cumming and William E. Henry, *Growing Old: The Process of Disengagement.* New York, Basic Books, 1961.

Simone de Beauvoir, *The Coming of Age.* New York, G. P. Putnam's Sons, 1972.

Helena Lopata, *Widowhood in an American City.* Cambridge, Mass., Schenkman, 1973.

Jeremy Tunstall, *Old and Alone.* London, Routledge & Kegan Paul, 1966.

CHAPTER 17

Ethical Conclusions

We see egotism versus altruism as the basic ethical problem in family life. Like all phenomena that we have tried to elucidate, it has the characteristic of bipolarity. The very helplessness with which human beings come into existence makes egotism a necessary reaction to their condition and to the surrounding world of possible resources. If one does not have the capacity to help oneself, there is no alternative to demanding and receiving. On the other hand, if other people do not stand ready to give without immediate reward, it is unlikely that human beings in infancy would receive sufficient nurture to maintain life or to develop satisfactorily. We see, therefore, from the beginning an interplay between egotism and altruism, between child and child rearer. But we must not forget that the child rearer was once a child and will, as an adult, have residues of egotism. Since in all likelihood many children will have to become child rearers directly or indirectly, they will have to develop altruism to maintain the proper existence of the human condition.

Socialization is essentially a process in which we try to help human beings to give up egotism and develop altruism in relation to the developmental phases in which people find themselves. Thus, altruism and egotism seen to have conflicting moralities. Actually, much internal conflict is a conflict between an original egotism which persists and the incorporation of altruism which socialization has produced.

Historically we have the heritage of altruistic morality largely due to the self-denying characteristic of Christian ideals. This is brought to extreme institutionalization in the monastic orders with their vows of poverty, obedience, and chastity. A less egotistical conduct of life can hardly be imagined. In family life we have the tradition of paternal and filial duties, which means that family life is the interplay of sacrifice on all sides. Currently the trend of perceptions of morality is clearly away from the idealization of sacrifice and the high value put on altruism; instead there is the striving toward the ideal of self-realization and, in consequence, the idealization of egotism. In the dominant lifestyle today a search for authenticity requires a ranking of values in which self comes before others. The morality of self-expression cannot consider others. If it does, it will very soon find itself handicapped and on the road back to sacrifice and to the loss of authenticity, a feeling of rightness in the world which family life rarely permits. A woman who is searching for self-realization in the marketplace cannot accept confinement within the domestic realm. A man who wants to change his job because he feels the deadening grip of routine cannot put family-income security above his search for a more meaningful job. An adolescent who expects to find self-realization in the non-academic world cannot, in terms of his morality, continue to go to school merely in order to please his parents or simply to live up to the expectations that children go to school without interruption.

In the long run, we must ask which morality, egotism or altruism, corresponds better to human needs? If problems cannot be seen in long-term perspective, at least which type of morality fits family life best at a certain period? A substantial number of people have chosen in the past and, with greater awareness, now choose singlehood, not as an intermediate stage between having been a child in the family created by their parents and the family which they created through their marriage, but as a permanent way of life. At present, more people are making this choice not only with greater awareness but for increasingly different reasons. Language has always had names for such people. Spinsters and bachelors are not newcomers to society. Existentialism has only given a philoso-phical foundation to an egotistical orientation toward family relationships which has existed long before the term "existential-ism" or the system of thought which it designates came into existence.

Problems, however, gain power from being conceptualized. Singlehood is now a greater problem—and for more people—than it used to be. It also creates problems for people who have decided not to spend their lives in singlehood because it makes family relationships conflict-ridden. In addition, there is the problem of reconciling one's own egotism with the demands of a social system in which one finds oneself involved out of the need to overcome loneliness, the need for permanency in intimacy, and the need for reproduction. There is also the possibility that one may simply need to do what the majority of people are doing and, therefore, may desire to meet the majority expectations which still favor marriage as a lifestyle for adults without being willing to change one's egotistical orientation.

We, however, do not believe that this experience of conflict is essential to family life in modern terms. We see it rather as a problem of contrasting the prevailing mood of relating to other people with the requirements of the various developmental phases of the human life cycle. Family life means family ties, and ties involve an inevitable sacrifice of freedom. Family life can therefore be seen as a stifling experience of being "glued together." However, it can also be seen as the ultimate in physical and emotional union for human beings.

Actually, people define and perpetuate their familial experience by the label they give to it. If one experiences family life as being "glued together" one is, in a manner of speaking, producing the glue. If one sees family life as an intermittently gratifying search for union and relief of loneliness, one will continue to find union a repetitive reward in family life. The dichotomy which we have presented here, however, should not blind us to the realization that even in singlehood, people will need the experience of union and relief of loneliness. On the other hand, even for people who institutionalize their needs for union and relief of loneliness in family life, there will be times when relationship sacrifices will become hardships and will be experienced as such.

Both lifestyles require, therefore, an element of the other lifestyle in order not to become destructive. Since this book is a book on family life, the reader has been invited to focus on the compromises and sacrifices of family life rather than on those of singlehood. Our criterion for solving the problems created by family life must be viewed in terms of the development of the family as a unified system. This system serves the needs of people of different ages and different sexes, and enables them to cope with the challenges of the developmental stages in which not only they themselves but the other family members find themselves. Where egotism supports this development it is moral, but when egotism interferes with the development of the family system, we must consider it as harmful and immoral. The physiological and psychological development of children requires release in adulthood, and if parents do not let go of their children and, instead, turn their status into an effective force of restraint, we have a case of immorality in the parent-child relationship. When, on the other hand, middle-aged sons and daughters refuse to assume the caretaker role for their aged parents, we have the same situation of immorality.

Another way of putting this view of developmental morality is to say that if egotism becomes dysfunctional within the family, then the relationship with the family must make a transition to a new and more altruistic base in order to survive.

We are in essence confronted with two types of ethics differentiated according to the sacrifices they imply and involve. People who maintain egotism through all developmental phases as the directive criterion of their reaction to others will at one point or another experience dysfunctional results of their pervasive stance. People who cannot permit freedom within the family for the developmental needs of the membership will equally harvest difficulties, misery, and probably defeat in their attempt to maintain the status quo.

There can be no question that different human beings require different lifestyles in order to approximate a state of well-being which prevents despair or becomes a source of discomfort to others. The choice of either singlehood or family life implies the answer to the question, "Who am I, do I know myself, do I know which ethical position I can hold and live accordingly?" It also requires imagination to know what type of lifestyle corresponds to each ethical and moral stand that we believe to be congenial to our personalities.

On the positive side, singlehood represents the freedom and readiness to embark on new experiences and new encounters, freedom over the use of time, and freedom from the burden of the dependency of others. On the negative side, people who remain single may not always have someone to worry about them or attend to them. They may find that their needs for company and succor are sacrificed to every familial responsibility of their married friends. Above all, they will have brushes with frightening loneliness and, as time goes on, a noticeable lack of skill to find people to help them overcome this loneliness. It is probably the ineptness for finding a relationship when needed which is the highest price that one has to pay for freedom from family ties.

One could say that conversely, familial life represents the security of relationships and protection against loneliness. The relationships satisfy the need for company, the need for continuation, and the need for somebody who cares and attends to you when you are "down." Put quite simply, it entitles you to be dependent. On the negative side, if one is married and has children or even if one is married and is childless, one has given hostages to fate. It is not only one's own misfortune, one's own sickness, one's own lack of success which will be burdensome but also the sickness and sorrows of one's family members. One thus increases the sources of trouble in one's life. Every other family member's trouble will demand one's rescuing intervention, for which one may or may not be ready. One may not ever be lonely but one may be frequently over-demanded.

All that this really means is that there are no bargains in the process of taking an ethical position. Ethics always imply renunciation. The question is only, "What is being renounced?" The problem condenses itself therefore to the decision concerning which price one finds to be equitable and relatively easy to pay as compared with the price required by the other life style.

The Authors

Index